THE MINDFUL SCHOOL: THE PORTFOLIO CONNECTION

BY

KAY BURKE,
ROBIN FOGARTY,
AND
SUSAN BELGRAD

IRI/Skylight Publishing, Inc.
Palatine, Illinois

The Mindful School:
The Portfolio Connection
First Printing

Published by IRI/Skylight Publishing, Inc.
200 E. Wood St. Suite 274
Palatine, Illinois 60067
1-800-348-4474, 708-991-6300
FAX 708-991-6420

Creative Director: Robin Fogarty
Editors: Julia E. Noblitt, Heidi Ray, Sabine Vorkoeper, Amy Wolgemuth
Type Compositor: Donna Ramirez
Book Designer: Bruce Leckie
Graphic Designer: David Stockman
Production Coordinators: Amy Behrens, Maggie Trinkle

ISBN 0-932935-78-8
Library of Congress Catalog Card Number: 94-78532

1311-10-94

TABLE OF CONTENTS

ACKNOWLEDGMENTS

The Portfolio Connection, envisioned as "just a little book," soon took on the qualities of bread dough rising. It expanded a bit beyond, above, and around the originally designed parameters. The more we wrote, the more we realized the creative potential of portfolios and the excitement generated by their use. And, as with any effort of an expansive nature, many hands made the final product possible.

First and foremost, we wish to extend a heartfelt thank you to our family members, friends, and colleagues who encouraged us...and endured with us. Their support has been unselfish and unending.

We extend a genuine tribute to those closest to the trials and tribulations of editing, designing, and publishing the book. Many thanks to the editorial staff, artists, designers, and coordinators at IRI/Skylight whose energy, talents, and skills made our ideas come alive.

Finally, there are a number of practitioners in the field to whom we owe special thanks:

- Roz Brown, Director of Effective Teaching Program for the New York State United Teachers (NYSUT), for sparking the idea of "a little portfolio book" for New York State teachers

- Jim Bellanca, President of IRI/Skylight Publishing, Inc. for acting on the idea (as he always does)

- Carolyn Chapman, IRI/Skylight National Consultant, for her willingness to be the "first" to train with the book and manual

- NYSUT teacher/trainers for their feedback in Carolyn's and Kay's initial training sessions in New York

- IRI/Skylight and St. Xavier University instructors Bonnie Byrne, Sue Koch, Pam Lindberg, Elsie Stiffler, Terry Stirling, and many others whose students in the Field-Based Master's Program tried, shared, and validated many of our authentic assessment and portfolio ideas. We especially loved their creative rubrics!

- Durham Board Teachers in Ontario, Canada for their conversations and artifacts on portfolios

To all who made this "little book" possible, we are forever indebted.

Kay, Robin, and Susan

INTRODUCTION

Rationale

"Portfolios in classrooms today are derived from the visual and performing arts tradition in which they serve to showcase artists' accomplishments and personally favored works" (Zimmerman, 1993, p. 1).

Teachers are borrowing the artists' portfolios to support new educational practices that emphasize the students' role in constructing their own understanding and in assessing their own progress. Portfolios also allow students to use creativity and originality to display their work in ways traditional tests cannot. They provide more effective ways to measure academic skills and to make informal decisions about instruction (Zimmerman, 1993). Portfolios allow students to show their *process* and their *products* as well as to move learning from the abstract to the concrete.

The Portfolio Concept

Zimmerman (1993) points out that the portfolio concept is gathering momentum in education, but it is not a new concept. Graphic designers, artists, architects, investment brokers, performers, and models often use portfolios to organize their work and to showcase their skills and talents. The items in the portfolio provide concrete examples of what a person is capable of doing and, therefore, provide another dimension beyond the written résumé or a test of skills.

"Using portfolios for assessment is an idea that is gaining popularity across the curricula. With increased attention being given to whole-language learning, meaningful mathematics, thematic science, and cooperative learning, multiple-choice tests no longer seem adequate for measuring student abilities" (Hamm & Adams, 1991, p. 18).

Authentic Assessment

The portfolio has emerged as one of the more powerful tools for assessment and evaluation in education. *Assessment* is the process of gathering evidence of what a student can do and *evaluation* is the process of interpreting the evidence and making decisions based on it (Burke, 1993). *Authentic assessment* is a term used to describe real tasks that require students to *perform* and/or *produce* knowl-

The portfolio has emerged as one of the more powerful tools for assessment and evaluation in education.

edge rather than *reproduce* information others have discovered (Newmann cited in Stefonek, 1991). The assessment/evaluation process has become a major focus of school reform. Teachers recognize that standardized tests and traditional paper-and-pencil tests do not always capture what students understand and are capable of doing. They agree with Brown (1989) when he says, "The concept that testing is initiated externally from the students, separate from the learning process, and primarily aimed at determining whether inert knowledge is in students' short-term memories exercises far too much influence over school people today" (p. 115).

> **Performance assessments require students to "generate rather than choose a response."**

The emphasis today is shifting from standardized tests and traditional multiple-choice tests to alternative forms of assessment that require a "direct examination of student *performance* on significant tasks that are relevant to life outside of school" (Worthen, 1993, p. 445). Performance assessments require students to "generate rather than choose a response" (Herman, Aschbacher, & Winters, 1992, p. 2). Students need to perform a task, demonstrate a skill, show a process, or produce a product that shows what they know and can do rather than take a multiple-choice test that may only measure how well they can memorize or take tests.

"A valid assessment system provides information about the particular task on which students succeed or fail, but more important, it also presents tasks that are worthwhile, significant, and meaningful—in short, *authentic*" (Archbald & Newmann, 1988, p. 1).

Experts like Collins, Wiggins, Newmann, and others (as cited in Stefonek, 1991, p. 1) offer these characteristics of authentic assessment: meaningful tasks, clear standards, reflections, transfer, formative and integrative, emphasis on higher-order thinking, and quality performances as well as quality products. (See Figure 1.)

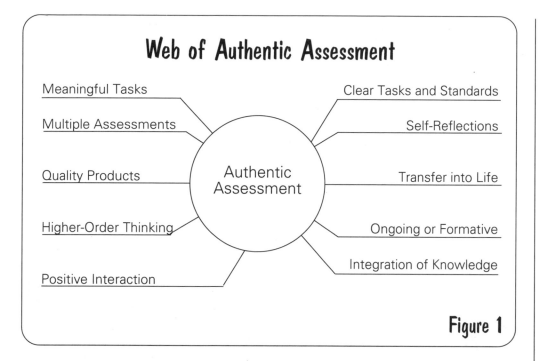

Web of Authentic Assessment

Meaningful Tasks

Multiple Assessments

Quality Products

Higher-Order Thinking

Positive Interaction

Authentic Assessment

Clear Tasks and Standards

Self-Reflections

Transfer into Life

Ongoing or Formative

Integration of Knowledge

Figure 1

Repertoire of Assessments

Just as the artist chooses from an array of watercolors to paint her picture, the creative teacher chooses from a repertoire of assessment tools to paint her picture of a student as a lifelong learner. Both works of art require planning, organization, careful selection, and frequent pauses to step back and view the "work in progress" from afar to see if the colors are "working" before the picture is finally finished. The more varied the colors, the more vivid the picture; the more varied the assessments, the more meaningful the evaluation.

Portfolio as a Palette

The artist's palette serves as an organizer for all the various paints, just as a portfolio serves as an organizational palette for all the authentic assessment tools. The portfolio pulls all the "loose ends" together to paint a picture of the whole student—not just an isolated or fragmented picture of the student. "A portfolio is more than just a container full of stuff. It's a systematic and organized collection of evidence used by the teacher and student to monitor growth of the student's knowledge, skills, and attitudes in a specific subject area" (Vavrus, 1990, p. 48).

Teachers need to select from an assortment of "different tints of paints" to motivate students and to help them understand important concepts and learning processes, regardless of their cultural diversity,

The portfolio pulls all the "loose ends" together to paint a picture of the whole student—not just an isolated or fragmented picture of the student.

ability levels, behavior dispositions, or socioeconomic backgrounds. The richer the palette, the more chances the students will have to appropriately demonstrate their skills, explore their talents, and discover knowledge for themselves. (See Figure 2.)

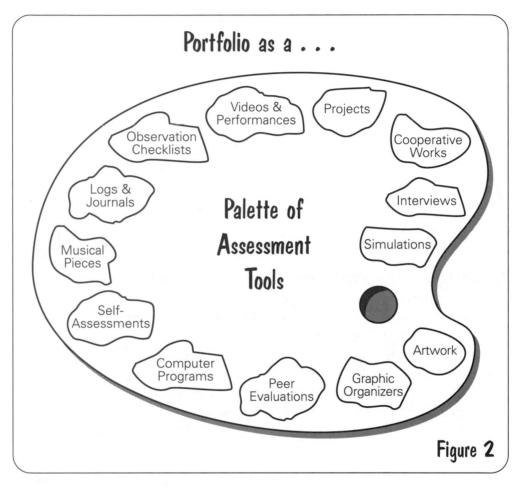

Portfolio as a . . .

Palette of Assessment Tools

Videos & Performances · Projects · Observation Checklists · Cooperative Works · Logs & Journals · Interviews · Musical Pieces · Simulations · Self-Assessments · Computer Programs · Peer Evaluations · Graphic Organizers · Artwork

Figure 2

While a standardized test score is only a "snapshot" of a student on a particular day, a portfolio shows how the student's work evolves over time.

What Is a Portfolio?

A portfolio can be both a container of evidence of a student's skills and a portrait of a student's development through the school year. While a standardized test score is only a "snapshot" of a student on a particular day, a portfolio shows how the student's work evolves over time. Paulson, Paulson, and Meyer (1991) and the Northwest Evaluation Association (a group of teachers from seven states) formulated this definition: "A portfolio is a purposeful collection of student work that exhibits the student's efforts, progress, and achievements in one or more areas. The collection must include student participation in selecting contents, the criteria for selection, the criteria for judging merits, and evidence of student self-reflection" (p. 60).

Purposes and Types

The variety of portfolio types used today is exciting. Teachers, like artists, are adopting the portfolio concept to accomplish educational goals, meet standards, or showcase student work.

PROPEL, a three-way consortium that includes the Pittsburgh Public Schools, The Educational Testing Service, and Project Zero at the Harvard Graduate School of Education, has developed portfolios to assess the thinking processes characteristic of the arts and humanities (Wolf, 1989). Students create biographies of their works as they collect a variety of artifacts, and reflections about them.

Campbell (1992) recommends using a laser disk portfolio assessment system that consists of a computer, CD-ROM drive, optical drive, scanner, and laser printer. The laser disks contain large amounts of information but the disks are small enough to fit into any student's permanent file.

Frazier and Paulson (1992) recommend using portfolios to motivate reluctant writers and make them the primary stakeholders in their writing.

Hansen (1992) advocates that students and teachers create Literacy Portfolios to help them know themselves as writers, readers, and artists, both inside and outside of school. Students include writings, lists of books they have read, favorite books, pictures, photos, report cards as well as comments or reflections about what an item means and why it was selected. They also include a list of goals and the artifacts that prove they have accomplished their goals.

The portfolio is a flexible and valuable tool that can be used for a variety of purposes. There can be as many types of portfolios as there are types of schools, classes, teachers, and students. The multitude of options are discussed further in Chapter One.

It may be acceptable for an artist to use only a handful of colors when he paints a portrait. But isn't the portrait more vivid and colorful if he uses a variety of the colors in his palette? It may be acceptable for a teacher to use only a handful of teaching strategies and assessments in the classroom. Some students will do well. But if a teacher uses a wide variety of motivating instructional strategies and evaluation tools, learning will come alive and be more relevant for all

The portfolio is a flexible and valuable tool that can be used for a *variety of purposes*.

students regardless of their learning styles or ability levels. Portfolios reveal how all students can be talented and gifted in different ways.

Despite the organizational headaches, storage problems, and time commitments, the educational benefits of using portfolios in the classroom far outweigh the logistical problems. Educators are starting to explore portfolios and to use them as a major assessment tool. Portfolios give teachers insights into their students and also help students take charge of their own learning. (See Figure 3.)

Despite the organizational headaches, storage problems, and time commitments, the educational benefits of using portfolios in the classroom far outweigh the logistical problems.

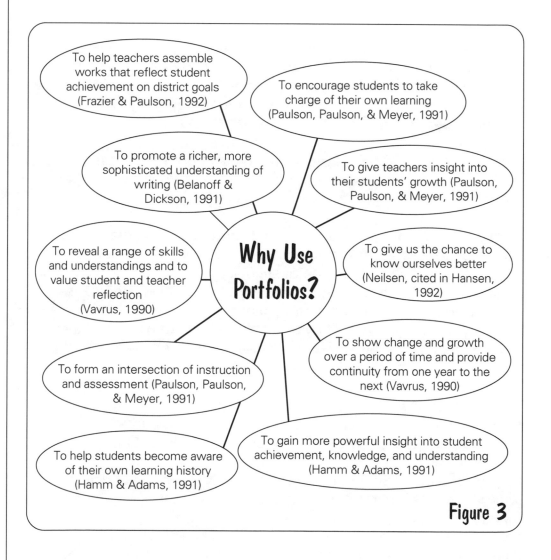

Figure 3

The Portfolio Process

The richness of the portfolio as an assessment tool is evident. The questions faced by educators all over the country are: How do I start? What goes in it? How will I use it? Where do I store it? How do I grade it? Does it follow the child from year to year? These nitty-gritty questions must be answered before beginning a portfolio system. There are no set answers to these questions or any other questions teachers may have. However, many options are available. Individual teachers, teams of teachers, entire faculties, and the district personnel must make some key decisions *before* they begin implementing a portfolio system. Of course, other minor organizational decisions will follow as the process evolves and becomes more refined. (See Figure 4.)

The Portfolio Process

1. Project the purposes and types of portfolios.

2. Collect and organize artifacts over time.

3. Select key artifacts based on criteria.

4. Interject personality through signature pieces.

5. Reflect metacognitively on each item.

6. Inspect to self-assess and align to goals.

7. Perfect and evaluate…and grade if you must.

8. Connect and conference with others.

9. Inject and eject artifacts continually to update.

10. Respect accomplishments and show with pride.

Figure 4

Individual teachers, teams of teachers, entire faculties, and the district personnel must make some key decisions *before* they begin implementing a portfolio system.

The following chapters address ten key issues and strategies that are part of *a portfolio system*. This book is designed around these ten elements that comprise the portfolio system. (See Figure 5.)

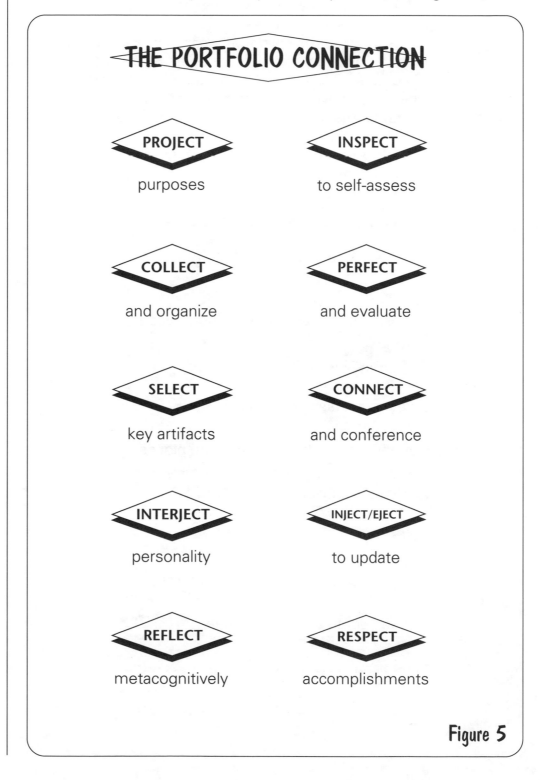

THE PORTFOLIO CONNECTION

PROJECT
purposes

INSPECT
to self-assess

COLLECT
and organize

PERFECT
and evaluate

SELECT
key artifacts

CONNECT
and conference

INTERJECT
personality

INJECT/EJECT
to update

REFLECT
metacognitively

RESPECT
accomplishments

Figure 5

Although the portfolio system, naturally, is a process that may or may not follow logically in the order outlined, an elaboration of each element, following the progression set in Figure 5, is meant to clarify the expectations inherent in the ten phases. Let's begin at the beginning and proceed accordingly.

Project Purposes

Early in the process, teachers look at the purposes for using portfolios. They examine the "big picture" and project possible uses and abuses as they decide on the type of portfolio to develop. *Projecting is focusing.*

Collect and Organize

A critical element of the portfolio system is the collection and organization of the artifacts. Teachers need to plan how to store all the artifacts and design tools that help students to organize their portfolios. *Collection is abundance.*

Select Key Artifacts

Another crucial phase in portfolio development is selecting key items. At this stage, teachers decide what the contents of the portfolio will be; who will select items; how often the artifacts will be prioritized; and how the selection will be done. *Selection is abandonment.*

Interject Personality

This phase calls attention to the person behind the portfolio by interjecting personality into the cover and page layouts of the portfolio; but interject is not an essential element. By including what is often referred to as "signature pieces," the student presents a profile of him- or herself and often the portfolio takes on a life of its own. Interjection focuses on including the personal touch of the individual students. *Interjection is style and flair.*

Reflect Metacognitively

The reflection phase requires the student to thoughtfully examine each piece selected for inclusion in the portfolio. Each artifact is carefully labeled to reflect its meaning and value to the student. By giving voice to why an artifact is included, students begin to know themselves introspectively. *Reflection is a mirror into the self.*

By giving voice to why an artifact is included, students begin to know themselves introspectively.

Inspect to Self-Assess

In addition to reflecting on each artifact, students also are expected to inspect their portfolio to assess themselves and their work. Have they met their long-term and short-term goals? Are their strengths and weaknesses evidenced? Does their portfolio indicate growth in the areas they targeted? Are they on track? *Inspecting ensures one is on course.*

Perfect and Evaluate

As portfolios become accepted assessment tools, the need for systematically perfecting them, fine-tuning the content, and getting them ready for the grading process is almost a given. *Perfecting is to make a polished final draft or a finished product.*

Connect and Conference

A natural progression of portfolio development is to share the finished product with someone. The portfolio conference provides the format for meaningful dialogue among students, teachers, and parents. It's a chance to connect with others, using the portfolio as the basis for discussion. *Connecting is conversing.*

Inject/Eject to Update

> **The portfolio is kept manageable only when items are injected and ejected on a regular basis.**

The inject/eject stage is similar to a revolving door—some things are added while others are taken out. The portfolio is kept manageable only when items are injected and ejected on a regular basis. This stage is not only necessary but desirable; the honing keeps the portfolio fresh. *Injecting/ejecting is the cycle of the portfolio.*

Respect Accomplishments

While this stage is not critical, formally exhibiting the portfolio adds a rich dimension to the portfolio process. As students prepare to exhibit, they target their audience, organize their material, rehearse within set time frames, and generally bring the project to a roaring culmination. *Respecting is celebration.*

As you progress through the book, or dip in and out of chapters of interest and need, please note that each chapter provides options, examples, and opportunities to formulate plans. Educators who have never used a portfolio can learn how to start using them. Beginners may choose to incorporate only the three essential steps: collect, select, reflect. Or they may want to elaborate a bit and use the six steps of the expanded model: project, collect, select, reflect, perfect, and connect. Educators who are already using portfolios can discover ways to refine and expand their use. They may want to include all ten steps of the elaborated model or select accordingly and tailor the process to their needs and expectations.

To clarify the three options of models for The Portfolio Connection, please refer to the chart in Figure 6.

Three Options for Portfolio Development

Essential Portfolio

Collect
Select
Reflect

Expanded Portfolio

Project
Collect
Select
Reflect
Perfect
Connect

Elaborated Portfolio

Project	Inspect
Collect	Perfect
Select	Connect
Interject	Inject/Eject
Reflect	Respect

Figure 6

The portfolio is the palette of potentiality, progress, and process.

Truly, the portfolio brings together not only instruction and assessment but also important elements from home, school, college, and work. It links the scantron tests of traditional evaluation to the hands-on application and transfer of knowledge necessary for future evaluations. The portfolio is the palette of potentiality, progress, and process. It is a body of work that represents the person, builds self-esteem, and provides a sense of accomplishment and pride. When the student sits down with a peer, teacher, or parent for a portfolio conference and says, "Let me show you my work and tell you about me," assessment becomes more than the multiple-choice test on Friday, it becomes a means to become a lifelong learner.

CHAPTER 1:

PROJECT
PURPOSES

"We think in generalities, we live in detail."
—Alfred N. Whitehead (cited in Peter, 1977, p. 493)

PROJECT PURPOSES

Overview

Portfolios are among the most frequently mentioned alternatives in the current repertoire of authentic assessment tools. However, portfolios are used sporadically and their purposes are still being defined. Yet, just as experienced by an artist, once an image appears in the mind's eye and the projections are actually visualized, the picture unfolds naturally. This is also true with the possibilities of portfolio use. Once the key players establish the primary purposes for using portfolios to assess learning, the actual implementation unfolds gradually and naturally.

Before introducing portfolios as assessment tools, it is critical that teachers look at the "big picture" to determine the primary and secondary uses of portfolios. They need to ask the hard questions: Why involve students in the ongoing process of gathering artifacts of their work throughout a year or semester? How are portfolios going to be used? What is the real purpose of this tool? What are the potential uses, overuses, and abuses of portfolios for assessment purposes and beyond?

Critical decisions must be made to determine the use of portfolios. Once this discussion takes place and the principal players agree on *how* and *why* to do portfolios, the project can be initiated with the students; at this point the goals and purposes are clear to all.

> **"Portfolios have the potential to reveal a lot about their creators. They can become a window into the students' heads."**

Introduction

"Portfolios have the potential to reveal a lot about their creators. They can become a window into the students' heads, a means for both staff and students to understand the educational process at the level of the individual learner. They can be powerful educational tools for encouraging students to take charge of their own learning. . . . If carefully assembled, portfolios become an intersection of instruction and assessment; they are not just instruction or just assessment, but, rather, both. Together, instruction and assessment give more than either give separately" (Paulson, Paulson, & Meyer, 1991, p. 61). (See Figure 7.)

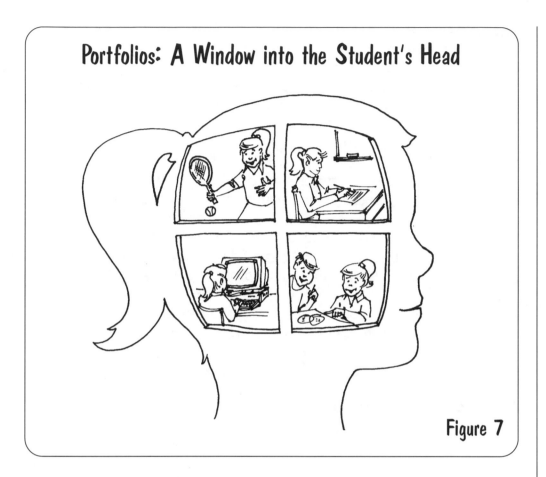

Portfolios: A Window into the Student's Head

Figure 7

A portfolio is... a *process* that enables students to become active and thoughtful learners.

Product and Process

A portfolio is more than just a final *product* students turn in to fulfill their course requirements. A portfolio is also a *process* that enables students to become active and thoughtful learners. The process of students collecting and selecting items to include in the portfolio and reflecting on their own learning makes portfolios powerful tools.

Three Principles of Assessment

Teachers and schools need to address three important principles of assessment when determining their purposes for using portfolios—content, learning, and equity. These principles were developed by the Mathematical Science Education Board (cited in Bass, 1993, p. 32).

The Content Principle

If teachers are accountable for student success in traditional content areas such as English, mathematics, science, and social studies, then assessments included in the portfolio reflect the *subject matter* that is important for students to learn.

The Learning Principle

If teachers have shifted focus from content to enabling students to become active and thoughtful learners through integrated curricula, then assessments included in the portfolio reflect the *learning processes* of reading, writing, speaking, listening, problem solving, and higher-order thinking.

The Equity Principle

If teachers recognize the importance of ensuring the success of ethnically and linguistically diverse students as well as students who are physically, behaviorally, or neurologically challenged, then assessments included in the portfolio *accommodate diversity*. Students demonstrate their learning through a wide variety of learning styles, multiple intelligences, and authentic communications.

Of course, many teachers combine all three of these purposes in portfolios in order to reflect content, process, and individuality.

Ideas

Purposes of Portfolios

Aligned with the principles of content, learning processes, and diversity, portfolios may target some or all of the following purposes.

Student Self-Assessment—"Mirrored Reflections"

Wolf (1989) asserts that one purpose of the portfolio is to have students learn to assess their own progress as learners. When students review and reflect on their work, they engage in the self-assessment process that fosters lifelong learning. The primary purpose of this type of portfolio is metacognitive reflection—the student monitors and celebrates his or her own growth and development.

Three Assessment Principles:
- **Content**
- **Learning**
- **Equity**

Mrs. Grimm, should we answer what is right, or what we think you think is right?!

Meet District or State Goals—"The State of Things"
Portfolios may comprise evidence that students have met learning goals. Usually the items are mandated (by the school, district, or state) and scoring rubrics are generated to measure the validity and reliability of the assessments. The student's work is assessed according to accepted benchmarks or exemplars (outstanding examples) that set standards, criteria, and indicators for each score.

Multiple Purposes—"Many Things to Many People"
A single portfolio may have multiple purposes. The power of the multiple portfolio is its versatility. Educators may construct a portfolio that includes content, learning processes, projects that encourage development of learning styles and multiple intelligences, evaluation based on district or state goals, and tools for student self-assessment. The multiple purpose portfolio draws from a diverse palette and provides a portrait of a student that is rich in texture, tone, and beauty.

Teacher Accountability—"Teacher Introspection"
Teachers may use portfolios to assess their own teaching to make sure they are accomplishing their goals and achieving the important objectives or outcomes of the course. Sometimes the student portfolios are used to evaluate the effectiveness of the teacher in meeting school or district goals.

Types of Portfolios

Once the central purposes for implementing a portfolio system have been determined, teachers and principals then consider what type of portfolio can best achieve these purposes. The following types may be used by themselves or in combination with other ideas to fulfill the purposes of the portfolio. These types fall into three distinct categories: personal, academic, or professional.

PERSONAL PORTFOLIOS

The Total Portfolio—"Me, Myself, and I"
Items from outside of school may be included in this portfolio to form a more holistic picture of the students. The entire portfolio may also be devoted to students' hobbies, community activities, musical or artistic talents, sports, families, pets, or travels. The portfolio might include artifacts, pictures, ribbons, awards, videos, or other memorabilia. Students might include either a written or videotaped autobiographical sketch, career or college goals, future travel or family plans, and reflections on what they need to accomplish to

> **The multiple purpose portfolio draws from a diverse palette and provides a portrait of a student that is rich in texture, tone, and beauty.**

make their dreams or career plans a reality. This type of portfolio allows classmates and the teacher to know more about students and to celebrate their interests and successes outside the traditional confines of the school.

My Best Work—"The Top Ten List"

The "best work" portfolio, popular at the elementary school level, includes items that may or may not have been graded previously. The purpose of this type of portfolio is to allow students to select entries from all the work they have done. (The selection process is discussed at length in Chapter Three.) Emphasis is given to "student choice." Once the teacher and the students have selected key items, they can review the work and see the students' growth and development.

ACADEMIC PORTFOLIOS

The Graded Portfolio—"To Grade or Not to Grade"

The graded portfolio includes several options:

1. *None* of the specific items in the portfolio may be graded. They have been graded before they become a part of the portfolio.
2. *Some* of the items may be graded. Usually teachers select two or three items and the student selects two or three items. About half of all the items will be scored for the final grade and the other items will be counted for completeness only.
3. *All* of the items in the final portfolio may be graded separately on the basis of predetermined criteria and scoring rubrics. (Rubrics are discussed in Chapter Seven.)
4. The *whole* portfolio may be given a grade based on criteria such as originality of cover, organization, reflectiveness, self-evaluation, and short-term and long-term goals. (Examples of how to grade a portfolio are provided in Chapter Seven.)

The Integrated Portfolio—"The Portfolio Connection"

The purpose of the integrated portfolio is to allow the students, teacher, and parents to view the "whole" student by seeing a body of work from all the disciplines and to show *connections* between or among the subjects included. The students select items from several or all of their subjects. The students may write reflections about their best or least favorite subjects and discuss what concepts or skills cross over into several subject areas and outside of the school setting.

None of the items may be graded. *Some* of the items may be graded. *All* of the items may be graded. The *whole portfolio* may be graded.

Cooperative Group Portfolio—"The Dream Team"

Each member of the cooperative group contributes individual items that showcase individual strengths. Group items—samples or pictures of group projects, performances, team-building activities, and school or community projects—may be included to demonstrate the power of the cooperative group. Preestablished criteria may be used to evaluate the group portfolio or the portfolio may be used for reflection and self-evaluation of the team's work. These group portfolios may also be used for conferences with other groups, teachers, and parents. The major purpose of a group portfolio is to emphasize the different strengths and talents heterogeneously grouped students bring to a group effort and to emphasize the importance of collaboration and interpersonal abilities as life skills.

Multi-Year Portfolio—"Days of Our Lives"

Some schools cluster grade levels together in either two-, three-, or four-year intervals and ask the students to save pieces from each year. For example, students save items from kindergarten, first, and second grade in different colored folders. These separate folders are then kept in a bigger folder (accordion or notebook) and stored at the school. Periodically, the students get out all their work and reflect on how much they have improved over the three-year period. They also ask fellow students to make comments on their progress in writing, reading (cassettes from each year), artwork, problem solving, and handwriting. The students really appreciate their progress when they see how much they have improved in three years. (Adapted from Crow Island School in Winnetka, IL.)

Multiple Intelligences—"My Seven Selves"

Schools that seek to ensure the success of students with diverse needs and learning styles use multiple intelligences portfolios to showcase all aspects of the students' talents. The portfolios include activities and assessments from Gardner's (1983) intelligences—visual/spatial, logical/mathematical, verbal/linguistic, musical/rhythmic, interpersonal, intrapersonal, and bodily/kinesthetic.

The Class Profile—"Touch of Class"

Each class compiles items that reflect the accomplishment and personality of the class as a whole. These items may include a class picture, motto, or song; class predictions; last wills and testaments for the next class; pictures or videos of class or community projects, performances, field trips, assemblies, or guest speakers; letters from parents, administrators, congressional representatives, business

The major purpose of a group portfolio is to emphasize the different strengths and talents heterogeneously grouped students bring to a group effort and to emphasize the importance of collaboration and interpersonal abilities as life skills.

7

leaders, or sports or movie personalities. The class portfolio may also include group projects or examples of team-building or bonding activities that have helped to bring the class together. Class poems, stories, biographical information, class profiles, computer programs, accomplishments, short- or long-term goals, career choices, or a collage of famous people in the news or of students in the class may provide a complete overview of the class.

Portfolios of Intelligent Behavior—"I Am a Thoughtful Learner"
Teachers who seek to promote intelligent and socially responsible behaviors use portfolios to focus on evidence of persistence, empathic listening, flexibility in thinking, metacognitive awareness, problem posing, and problem solving (Costa, 1991).

The Schoolwide Profile—"Be True to Your School"
A schoolwide portfolio is kept by principals and staff members to chronicle the school year. Entries in the portfolio could include schoolwide events such as Campus Beautification Day, Field Day, or thematic events such as School Olympics or International Day. Pictures or videos of sporting events, special speakers, assemblies, schoolwide awards, field trips, class trips, honor rolls, plays, parties, PTA/PTO nights, National Merit or Scholarship winners, student or teacher awards, science fair projects, or performances are included along with reflections and observations. The observations or reflections are contributed by students, teachers, parents, or administrators. The school portfolio is kept in the school office or media center for people to review.

Time Capsule Portfolio—"The Dig"
The students can also select key artifacts and write predictions for the future and bury them in a time capsule to be dug up in five or ten years. Once a cycle is started, schools may want to bury a time capsule and dig one up each year to symbolize the connections between classes and generations. The time capsule portfolio documents the history of a school for future generations.

Districtwide Profile—"The Big Picture"
Districts can keep a cumulative portfolio that contains contributions from each of the schools as well as districtwide events such as science fairs, book fairs, community projects, scores on standardized tests, National Merit winners, scholarship winners, schools of excellence, physical fitness awards, state or federal grants, computer innovations, and students, teachers, and administrators who have

> **The time capsule portfolio documents the history of a school for future generations.**

won awards. The districtwide portfolio also includes evidence to show how the district has met accreditation requirements or state goals or outcomes in assessment, test scores, or special education. This type of portfolio may be used to plan instruction or programs based on an evaluation of a district's strengths and weaknesses.

PROFESSIONAL PORTFOLIOS

College Admissions Portfolio—"Prepfolio"

Colleges and universities may ask a prospective freshman to prepare a portfolio that contains samples of his or her work in high school. The college admissions and placement personnel review evidence of the student's abilities in all subject areas and extracurricular and community activities to determine how a student may contribute to the college. Some colleges use the portfolio as part of the acceptance process because it adds a richer dimension to grade point averages and standardized test scores. Other colleges use the portfolio for placement in academic courses once the students have been accepted.

College Scholarships—"Scholarly Folio"

Students compile portfolios that contain their academic transcripts, attendance and discipline records, standardized test scores, and other pertinent information for eligibility for scholarships. They also include letters of recommendation, commendations, videos, news stories, programs, yearbooks, playbills, and any other information to show why the student should be considered for academic or athletic scholarships.

Employability Portfolio—"Working Papers"

Some schools, school districts, and states require students to collect evidence of their employability skills. The student is asked to show his or her academic work as well as evidence of his or her ability to communicate, to work in a group, and to work responsibly. Often, the student is asked to compile a portfolio for a mock job interview. She practices interview techniques and dresses appropriately for the interview. During the interview the student discusses the contents of her portfolio and explains why she would make a good employee. Members of the business community often participate in these mock interviews and critique a student's performance by telling her whether or not they would hire her based on her portfolio, résumé, presentation, and interview.

Some schools, school districts, and states require students to collect evidence of their employability skills.

Preservice Portfolio—"Intern Returns"

Some undergraduate education programs require student teachers to keep a portfolio of their training and teaching experiences. This portfolio contains lists of courses taken, sample lesson plans, reading lists, artifacts from students' work, samples of extracurricular activities, videos or cassettes of lessons, interviews with students, workshops or seminars attended, evidence of peer coaching, copies of evaluations, letters from students and parents, long-term goals, and self-evaluations of their teaching experience. Some student teachers also keep ongoing logs and journals of their teaching experiences along with personal reflections and feedback from supervising teachers, mentors, or college supervisors.

The portfolio may count toward the students' teaching grade, but it can also be used for job interviews. Prospective employers are interested in teacher performance. Some now require teachers to bring a portfolio to the initial interview. Many principals or directors of personnel also want to know if potential employees have experience in innovative educational strategies. For example, if the district emphasizes cooperative learning, integrated curricula, positive discipline, multiple intelligences, or authentic assessment, they might prefer to hire teachers who already understand and practice the concepts rather than having to invest in additional staff development for new teachers.

Teacher Portfolio—"Teacher as Researcher"

Teachers model how to use personal and professional portfolios by compiling their own portfolios. The portfolio can include evidence of completed short- and long-term goals. For example, teachers may have a preconference with their supervisor and list cooperative learning as a goal for the next school year. The portfolio would then contain pictures, videos, lesson plans, and artifacts that validate that the teacher is implementing cooperative learning in his or her classroom. These artifacts can be used in the postconference to determine if the teacher fulfilled the stated goal by effectively using cooperative learning.

Staff Evaluation Portfolio—"How Am I Doing?"

Some districts use portfolio conferences to evaluate teachers instead of relying on one or two twenty-minute observations per year. The teacher portfolios may include videos of actual lessons; student work; test scores; self-assessments; seminars, inservices, or personal growth conferences; evidence of courses completed or addi-

The portfolio can include evidence of completed short- and long-term goals.

tional degrees earned; awards, honors, or commendations; letters from students, parents, or administrators; evidence of extracurricular or community involvement, hobbies, sports, or out-of-school activities; evidence of family involvement; short- and long-term goals; and philosophy of education.

Teacher Portfolio—"Job File"
Teachers who change jobs use the portfolio in the interview process; it provides a rich overview of the personality and ability of the teacher.

Administrator Portfolio—"Principal Principles"
Administrators may also compile evidence of their leadership abilities. The evidence includes schoolwide planning models; mission statements; examples of strategic or site-based planning meetings, or examples of innovative programs; commendations; examples of integrated units, schoolwide test scores, or financial records; and documentation of professional improvement such as course work, seminars, and inservices attended by the administrator or provided by the administrator for the staff. Employers and prospective employers may want evidence that the administrator has knowledge or experience in areas such as inclusion, detracking, cooperative learning, site-based management, total quality schools, higher-order thinking strategies, problem-based learning, integrated curricula, multiple intelligences, authentic assessment, consensus building, nongraded schools, or any other topics related to school restructuring that may be applicable to a district's goals. Since the school leader usually sets the tone for the whole school, district personnel may want to see evidence of an administrator's knowledge of and commitment to the best educational practices.

Performance Reviews—"It's My Job"
Some employers outside the school arena use portfolios as part of their employee performance review process. These portfolios include artifacts that indicate the employee's abilities and attitudes on the job and his or her personal reflections about the selections. They, in turn, provide the impetus for meaningful discussions about priorities, special tasks, quantity versus quality, and a variety of other fruitful paths of dialogue. In addition, the portfolio process allows employees the opportunity to take some ownership of the review process.

Teachers who change jobs use the portfolio in the interview process; it provides a rich overview of the personality and ability of the teacher.

11

Examples: Project Purposes—Types of Portfolios

PRIMARY

MULTI-YEAR PORTFOLIO

< Grades K-2 >

1. Cassette recording of student readings from each grade level.

2. Two drawings from each grade level.

3. Two samples of written work from each grade level (one from the beginning of the year; one from the end of the year).

4. A video that contains one oral presentation from each year.

5. A student-selected "best work" from each year.

MIDDLE SCHOOL

INTEGRATED PORTFOLIO

Integrates: language arts, social studies, math, science, art, music
Theme: Criminal Justice

1. Videotape of mock trial of Boo Radley in *To Kill a Mockingbird*.

2. Analysis of types of capital punishment from a medical perspective.

3. Graphs of the number of prisoners on death row in each state, their race, age, and level of education.

4. Journal entry on one day in the life of a death-row prisoner.

5. Sketches of scenes from a courtroom or prison.

6. Time lines of famous trials in American history.

HIGH SCHOOL

EMPLOYABILITY PORTFOLIO

1. Research on three different careers that includes the following:
   - type of training necessary
   - length of training
   - institutions that provide training
   - cost of training
   - anticipated salary

2. Video of a job interview.

3. A typed job résumé.

4. One collaborative group project.

5. List of hobbies, certificates, honors, special training, courses, or extra-curricular activities.

COLLEGE

BEST WORK PORTFOLIO

Subject: American Literature

1. Annotated bibliography of writers associated with the Harlem Renaissance.

2. Video of debate about which contemporary author deserves the Nobel Prize for Literature.

3. A Venn diagram comparing Edgar Allan Poe to Stephen King.

4. A critique of Hemingway's novel, *The Sun Also Rises*.

5. My Top Ten List of the best American women writers (and a rationale for their ranking).

TEACHER PLANNER

What are the *purposes* of my portfolio?
- Content Principle

  _____

  _____

- Learning Principle

  _____

  _____

- Equity Principle

  _____

  _____

What *type(s)* of portfolios do I plan to use? Why?_____

_____

_____

_____

What is my *time line* for implementation?_____

_____

_____

_____

What *questions* or concerns do I have?_____

_____

_____

_____

_____

©1994 by IRI/Skylight Publishing, Inc.

Blackline

MULTI-YEAR PORTFOLIO

My Portfolio Can Help Me to Tell My Story

Student Name _____   Date _____

1.   Label your work according to the grade level.
2.   Spread out the work by dates (earliest date to most current date).
3.   Select three writing assignments (one from each year).
4.   Line them up in order and review them carefully.
5.   Answer the following questions about your three samples:
     What major difference do you see?

     _____

     _____

     What surprised you the most?

     _____

     _____

     How have your interests changed?

     _____

     _____

     What skills (handwriting, grammar, spelling, organization, vocabulary,
     etc.) do you still need to develop more? Why?

     _____

     _____

6.   Show your three sample pieces to a peer. Ask for comments about
     any changes he or she sees.
     Peer Comments: _____

     _____

7.   Set new goals for yourself.
     Goal One: _____
     Goal Two: _____
     Goal Three: _____

(Adapted from Kate Smith, a teacher at Crow Island School in Winnetka, IL)

©1994 by IRI/Skylight Publishing, Inc.

Blackline

EMPLOYABILITY PORTFOLIO

Directions: Select items you could include in a portfolio to show to a prospective employer.

Name _____ Date _____

TABLE OF CONTENTS
ACADEMIC SKILLS

1. _____ page ____
2. _____ page ____
3. _____ page ____

RESPONSIBILITY SKILLS

4. _____ page ____
5. _____ page ____
6. _____ page ____

COOPERATIVE SKILLS

7. _____ page ____
8. _____ page ____
9. _____ page ____

©1994 by IRI/Skylight Publishing, Inc.

Blackline

NOTES:

_____

_____

_____

_____

_____

_____

_____

_____

_____

_____

_____

_____

_____

_____

_____

_____

_____

_____

_____

_____

_____

_____

CHAPTER 2:

COLLECT AND ORGANIZE

"All profoundly original art looks ugly at first."
—Clement Greensberg (cited in Peter, 1977, p. 29)

COLLECT AND ORGANIZE

Overview

Once the purposes of the portfolio are clearly defined, the process of developing a portfolio begins. Students start the ongoing process of gathering and collecting artifacts of their work for possible inclusion in their portfolios. Imagine for a moment an artist surrounded by the tools and supplies necessary for the creative process. An assortment of brushes, varying sizes of canvas, and of course, the array of colored paints are gathered conveniently around the easel as the artist readies herself to create a "masterpiece." What may appear to those on the outside as a somewhat cluttered studio is actually, upon closer view, a study in organization. Brushes are categorized by size and type, paints are sequenced by tints and tones, and the drawings and sketches are close at hand.

Organization and planning are as necessary for student portfolios as for creating masterpiece artwork. But like the artist, teachers and students are free to organize artifacts according to their creative instincts. Specific decisions about how to put things together for easy reference and logical continuity require a number of considerations including the type of container (notebook, box, bag, envelope, file folder, or photo album); the labeling technique (tabs, table of contents, registry); the order of things (sequential, prioritized, thematic, or random); and the overall look of the collection (academic, aesthetic, personal, or eclectic).

These preliminary organizational decisions shape the integrity of the portfolio. If order guides portfolio development in the early stages (when the number and variety of artifacts is manageable), then order will reign over chaos in the later stages (when the amount of material can easily become unmanageable). If order guides this process, students will know where to store items and, therefore, will be more likely to keep important artifacts. So this phase addresses two concerns: how to collect things and how to organize the things collected.

If order guides portfolio development in the early stages (when the number and variety of artifacts is manageable), then order will reign over chaos in the later stages (when the amount of material can easily become unmanageable).

Introduction

"A portfolio is a purposeful collection of student work that exhibits the student's efforts, progress, and achievements in one or more areas" (Paulson, Paulson, & Meyer, 1991, p. 60).

Most teachers realize that portfolios are rich tools for demonstrating what students know and can do in a class. They also believe portfolios are more effective than traditional paper-and-pencil tests for measuring academic skills and making informed instructional decisions. Their concern, however, usually focuses on logistics: "How is it possible to collect all the 'stuff' from all my students, organize it into a portfolio system, and still maintain my sanity?"

"How is it possible to collect all the 'stuff' from all my students, organize it into a portfolio system, and still maintain my sanity?"

Here, Mommy.

Portfolios do take more time and require a great deal more planning than the instructional methods (e.g., worksheets, questions at the end of the chapter, memorization of discrete facts) they replace. Meaningful portfolio projects *don't just happen*. Research shows that portfolios place additional demands on teachers and students as well as on school resources. Teachers, administrators, policy makers, and students must exercise considerable effort to develop a meaningful portfolio process and plan for confidentiality to respect the ownership and privacy of the portfolio.

Ideas

Even though a teacher may be a risk-taker, requiring 150 high school freshmen to keep a portfolio of their work takes courage and a great deal of planning. Most freshmen can collect "stuff" (just look at their bedroom closets or school lockers), but they may not be able to organize all of the loose ends. Teachers need to develop a plan to handle the logistics of an undertaking of this magnitude. There are many ways to organize a portfolio system, but the following options for storage, organizational flow, and organizational tools might help in the formulation of the plan.

Storage

Hanging Files—"Hang It Up"
Teachers may set up hanging files for all their students. They may start with a "working portfolio" that contains all the students' work and then move to a final portfolio that contains as few as ten entries. Students keep all of their work in the hanging file stored in a file cabinet, crate, or box.

Notebooks—"Book It"
Students in the upper grades could be required to keep a notebook that has dividers and folders for pieces of work. The pocket folder could hold artifacts, cassettes, or videos. Plastic protectors could be used for rough drafts as well as final copies. Both are included so that teacher and students may review the biography of a work or the process that goes into arriving at the final version.

Rainbow Collection—"Rainbowing"
Students may keep colored folders to separate their work according to subject areas, works in progress, best work, "not yet" work, group work, or integrated assignments. These folders may be stored in file cabinets, student desks, or student notebooks.

Accordion-Pleated Folders—"Accordion Pleats"
Often large folders are needed to contain big samples, artifacts, or projects. These folders can also hold cassette tapes, videos, computer disks, colored file folders, notebooks, and bigger group projects.

Cereal Boxes—"Snap, Crackle, Pop"
Elementary teachers may use large cereal boxes to hold student work. They can write the student's name on the side panel and store them upright on a shelf. The students may decorate the front and back of the boxes with artwork or collages and use them to store their work. The box then serves as a working portfolio before selected items are transferred to a final portfolio that contains between seven and ten items.

Media Center—"Bank Vault"
Class or schoolwide portfolios, integrated portfolios, or multi-year portfolios can be placed in accordion-pleated folders and stored in the media center for easy access and review. Students check out their portfolios as needed, especially for updates of the registry, revisions, and conferences.

Elementary teachers may use large cereal boxes to hold student work.

Photo Albums—"Snapshots"

Photo albums can be used for pictures of student projects, group skits, performances, field trips, extracurricular activities, the student's family pictures, commendations, awards, hobbies, travels, and letters from famous people; programs from school concerts or plays; write-ups from school or local newspapers; invitations to events; ticket stubs from sporting or cultural events; or anything that provides insight into a student's life, both inside and outside of school.

Computer Disks—"Disks"

Students may include written work, problem-solving logs, journals, and scripts on computer disks. Technology makes it possible to scan pictures and to record voices. Some schools also include contents of the cumulative folder such as test scores, emergency phone numbers, medical information, and special education individual evaluation programs on the computer disk. The accessibility of the contents of a computer disk portfolio should be monitored carefully for confidentiality.

> **The accessibility of the contents of a computer disk portfolio should be monitored carefully for confidentiality.**

Organizational Flow

Although a comprehensive portfolio incorporates ten steps, the three essential steps—collect, select, reflect—are crucial to the organizational flow of the portfolio. (See Figure 8.)

ORGANIZATIONAL FLOW FOR A PORTFOLIO SYSTEM

Collect
everything into the
working portfolio

Select
pieces for the final portfolio

Reflect
on your selections

Figure 8

The collection process can take two to ten weeks, a quarter, a semester, or a year, depending on the time frame of each class.

Working Portfolio—"Collectibles"

After students have *collected* all their work and stored it in an appropriate hanging file, notebook, cereal box, or container, the process is only one-third of the way completed. The collection process can take two to ten weeks, a quarter, a semester, or a year, depending on the time frame of each class. Once the collection stage is completed or anytime during the collection stage, the students need to move to the next level of portfolio development. (See Figure 9 for ideas about what students might collect.)

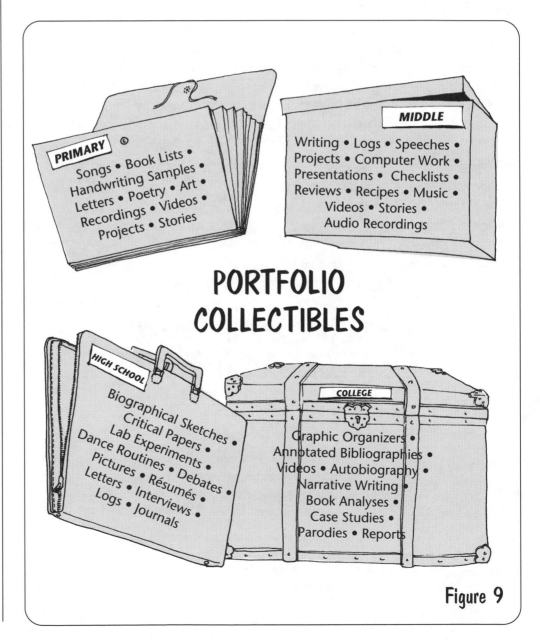

PORTFOLIO COLLECTIBLES

PRIMARY
Songs • Book Lists • Handwriting Samples • Letters • Poetry • Art • Recordings • Videos • Projects • Stories

MIDDLE
Writing • Logs • Speeches • Projects • Computer Work • Presentations • Checklists • Reviews • Recipes • Music • Videos • Stories • Audio Recordings

HIGH SCHOOL
Biographical Sketches • Critical Papers • Lab Experiments • Dance Routines • Debates • Pictures • Résumés • Letters • Interviews • Logs • Journals

COLLEGE
Graphic Organizers • Annotated Bibliographies • Videos • Autobiography • Narrative Writing • Book Analyses • Case Studies • Parodies • Reports

Figure 9

Final Portfolio—"Selectables"

The selection process is critical to the portfolio process. (Chapter Three discusses the options in the selection process in detail.) The selection process is determined by many things: the purpose of the portfolio, the audience, and the type of portfolio. Items may be selected by categories. For example, students may select two writing samples, one group project, one performance, one extracurricular entry, one best work, etc. Later in the portfolio process, students will have a chance to refine, reflect upon, and update their selections.

Final Portfolio—"Reflectibles"

Even though teachers may require that certain entries be included in the portfolios, students should be able to choose many of the items to be included. The reflection process is important because students verbalize or write about why they make the selections and how they feel about the piece. (Chapter Five reviews numerous ways students can share their feelings and thoughts through reflection.)

Organizational Tools

Dividers—"Tabs & Dabs"

Divided notebook folders or plastic divider pages can be used to separate work by genre, subject area, rough drafts, final drafts, best work, "not yet" work, individual work, or group work, or to divide the portfolio according to the table of contents. Tabs allow students and their audience quick access to specific pieces.

> The selection process is determined by many things: the purpose of the portfolio, the audience, and the type of portfolio.

COLORED DOT CODES

Green dot .... First draft
Yellow dot .... Second draft
Red dot .... Final draft
Blue dot.. Reflection
Orange dot .... Group work
Black dot .... "Not yet" work

Figure 10

Colored Dots—"Dotted Swiss"

Colored dots in all sizes can be used to code entries in the portfolio. The dots could be used in the working portfolio to help in the selection process or in the final portfolio to help with organization. A code for the dots is often included in the Table of Contents. (See Figure 10.)

Table of Contents—"Table It"

A portfolio may include a table of contents that lists all of the entries and page numbers. Most portfolios contain between seven and ten items. Several things like the reflection page, the student self-assessment, and the goal-setting page are necessary; the other items are representative of the student's work.

Artifact Registry—"Hotel Registry"

A portfolio registry chronicles when and why students remove items (eject) and replace them with newer items (inject) (Dietz, 1992). (See Chapter 9 for more information on the inject/eject phase.) Students record the dates, items, and reasons for the replacement. This ongoing process reinforces students' metacognition—thinking about their own thinking and learning processes. (A sample of the registry is on page 26.)

Self-Assessment Stems—"Me-Notes"

Students can make connections between their work and their personal goals by assessing their entire portfolio. They may base their self-assessments on their feelings about how much they have learned, how far they have progressed, or how much time and effort they put into their portfolio. They may also assess their work based upon predetermined criteria and indicators developed by the class. These scoring rubrics are based upon key criteria and the degree to which students meet the criteria. (See Chapter Seven, pages 90, 91, 93, and 96 for examples.)

Biography of a Work Log—"Bed to Bed"

Wolf (1989) says that long-term projects require "moment-to-moment monitoring, Monday morning quarterbacking, and countless judgments of errors and worth" (p. 35). A biography of a work can be used to trace the development of any worthwhile project. The biography may include dated entries that trace the development of an idea from its inception to the final product or performance—or metaphorically, getting up in the morning to going to bed in the evening (bed to bed). (See examples on pages 26 and 29.)

Index—"Let Your Fingers Do the Walking"

The index is another organizational tool for portfolios. Students can

A portfolio registry chronicles when and why students remove items (eject) and replace them with newer items (inject).

compile an alphabetical index of major items at the end of their portfolios. The index serves as an easy reference for anyone looking for specific examples that show evidence of writing skills, learning styles, multiple intelligences, group work, artwork, extracurricular activities, or subject content.

Feedback: Post-it Notes—"Note Post"
Students always want feedback on their work. Formal feedback may include a portfolio evaluation form or scoring rubric. Informal feedback may include comments written on Post-it notes. They may include memos, a poem, or a picture by a fellow student, parent, or teacher. And by using a Post-it note, the students' original work is not violated and the comments appear on "removable" notes.

Examples: Collect and Organize

STORAGE

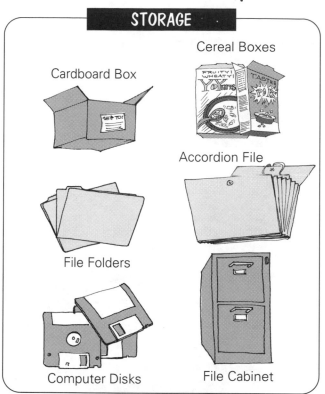

Cardboard Box

Cereal Boxes

Accordion File

File Folders

Computer Disks

File Cabinet

ORGANIZATIONAL FLOW

Working Portfolio (Hanging File, Notebook, Cereal Box)

↓

Collect Everything (Five to Seven Weeks)

↓

Final Portfolios (Folder, Computer Disk, Photo Album)

↓

Select Seven to Ten Items (One or Two Weeks)

↓

Reflect on Work (One Week)

↓

Hold Conferences (One Week)

TOOL

ARTIFACT REGISTRY

Name Mary S.　**Class** American Literature

DELETIONS

Date	Item	Reasons
3/5/94	Book report on *The Great Gatsby*	I didn't understand symbolism so I used Cliff Notes. Not my best work.
3/25/94	Sonnet on Sylvia Plath	I was so worried about a rhyme scheme that content suffered.

ADDITIONS

Date	Item	Reasons
3/5/94	Book report on *Tender Is the Night*	I liked this book by Fitzgerald better. I could figure out symbolism on my own.
3/25/94	Free verse poem on Plath	It didn't rhyme, but I said what I felt. More meaningful.

TOOL

BIOGRAPHY OF A WORK LOG

Group Project Present a Decade in History

Date	Log Entry
4/29/94	Group voted to pick the decade of the 1920s for presentation.
5/2/94	Brainstormed ideas for key elements of decade.
5/3/94	Went to media center to research key elements.
5/4/94	Divided key elements among 5 members: (1) Historical Events (4) Music (2) Politics (5) Art (3) Clothes
5/5-5/10/94	Gathered information, costumes, music, artifacts, newspaper headlines.
5/11-5/13/94	Wrote script for skit, made slides, selected music.
5/16/94	Presented retrospect of 1920s to the class.

Comments: Our group worked well together; we even learned the Charleston.

IRI SkyLight

TEACHER PLANNER

Storage

How will I *store* my portfolios?_____
_____
_____
_____

Organizational Flow

What is my *time line* for collecting, selecting, reflecting, and conferencing? ___
_____
_____
_____

Organizational Tools

What types of *tools* (table of contents, tabs, index) will I use to organize my portfolios?_____
_____
_____
_____

Questions

What *questions* or concerns do I have about the collection process?_____
_____
_____
_____

Confidentiality

How will I assure *confidentiality* in portfolio collection and storage?
_____
_____
_____

Blackline

ARTIFACT REGISTRY

Student_____ **Class**_____ **Date**_____

DELETIONS

Date	Item	Reasons

ADDITIONS

Date	Item	Reasons

IRI SkyLight

Blackline

BIOGRAPHY OF A WORK LOG

Student_____ **Date** _____ **Work**_____

Date	Log Entry

Comments:

Signed: _____

IRI
SkyLight

Blackline

NOTES:

_____
_____
_____
_____
_____
_____
_____
_____
_____
_____
_____
_____
_____
_____
_____
_____
_____
_____
_____
_____
_____
_____

CHAPTER 3:

SELECT
KEY ARTIFACTS

"Less is more."
—Mies Van Der Rohe (cited in Peter, 1977, p. 29)

SELECT KEY ARTIFACTS

Overview

Collection is to abundance as selection is to abandonment. Or, in the case of the artist, her palette must be carefully selected for the look, mood, and theme of the work. So too with the student portfolio. Artistic and academic decisions must be made about the context and contents of the portfolio based on the intent and purposes that the portfolio serve. Alignment to the goals and standards must be considered and attention given to the methodology used. At this stage, the artist determines the focal point of the work and proceeds accordingly.

Periodically, candidate artifacts must face the selection process. Decisions must be made. The final vote must be taken and some of the nominated items included, and others excluded. The selection process is activated as teachers and students preview, review, and establish relevant criteria. Let's take a look at the possibilities for action at the stage of making selections. They include decisions about what, how, who, and when.

The selection process is tightly linked to criteria and standards.

The selection process is tightly linked to criteria and standards. If criteria have been predetermined, artifacts must be matched to the established criteria and checked to see that the criteria are met. For example, are there representative pieces for each of the types of work required? In a writing portfolio, are there both narratives and expository pieces? business letters and journal entries? poetry, as well as literary critiques?

If criteria have not been predetermined or formalized, this is the time to discuss how to establish criteria and select pieces. Teachers must decide if general guidelines or more specific criteria are appropriate. Decisions are made about who selects artifacts and when selections are made. In any case, the selection process is critical in the development of student portfolios.

Introduction

"The crucial role of assessment is captured by the folk wisdom that you get what you assess and you do not get what you do not assess" (Bass, 1993, p. 32).

Once the *purpose* for the portfolio has been established and the *type* has been determined, it is time to select the items that will be included in the final portfolio. The portfolio selection process is correlated closely with the type of portfolio. For example, an employability portfolio would contain evidence of a student's potential in the work force. Lists of courses in a particular field, recommendations, a résumé, examples of work, and previous job experience would all be items that describe the student as a candidate for a job. All of the types of portfolios described in Chapter One dictate the selection of specific items that would demonstrate the person's understanding or expertise in a particular area.

The selection process, therefore, begins with several important questions about portfolios:
- *What* should be included?
- *How* will the items be selected?
- *Who* will select the items?
- *When* will these items be selected?

Ideas

What Should Be Included?
Selection is based on a variety of things. The focus may be on particular subject matter, various learning processes, the spectrum of multiple intelligences, or a special project or unit.

Subject- or Content-Area Learning—"Just the Facts"
Items that demonstrate what a student understands about a particular subject area like language arts, mathematics, science, or art would be included in a subject-area portfolio. For example, a portfolio for a language arts class could contain the following: book reports, key vocabulary words, a research paper, a response journal to a piece of literature, a letter to the editor, a poem, a panel discussion, a performance tape of a scene from a play, a reflection of the portfolio, a self-assessment, and a list of future goals. Students and teachers need to select the types of items that are representative of important concepts in subject areas.

Learning Process—"The Experience"
In this type of portfolio, teachers and students select items that represent the learning processes. The content is secondary because the focus is on skills and processes like speaking, listening, writing, reading, problem solving, decision making, or higher-order thinking skills.

> Once the *purpose* for the portfolio has been established and the *type* has been determined, it is time to select the items that will be included in the final portfolio.

The entries demonstrate the students' proficiency in these areas by written work, cassettes, and videos to demonstrate oral work, and teacher observations checklists and interviews with students.

Multiple Intelligences—"The Spectrum"

A multiple intelligence portfolio would include entries that represent the seven intelligences of the students.

A multiple intelligence portfolio would include entries that represent the seven intelligences of the students. The student might include logs, journals, and reflections to depict his verbal/linguistic and intrapersonal intelligences; a Venn diagram to depict his visual/spatial intelligence; a computer program to depict his logical/mathematical intelligence; a video of a group performance to depict his bodily/kinesthetic and interpersonal intelligences; and a rap song to represent his musical/rhythmic intelligence. Students can then *select* items that showcase their talents and explain why they feel they are strong in some areas and need work in others. This type of portfolio provides a wide variety of entries and demands that the student "stretch" his talents and expand his repertoire of products and processes. (See Figure 11 for a description of Gardner's seven intelligences and Figures 12 and 13 for how to select key items for the portfolio.)

THE SEVEN INTELLIGENCES

7 WAYS OF KNOWING

MULTIPLE INTELLIGENCES

LOGICAL/MATHEMATICAL INTELLIGENCE
Often called "scientific thinking," this intelligence deals with deductive thinking and reasoning, numbers, and the recognition of abstract patterns.

VISUAL/SPATIAL INTELLIGENCE
This intelligence relies on the sense of sight and the ability to visualize an object and to create mental images/pictures.

BODILY/KINESTHETIC INTELLIGENCE
This intelligence relates to physical movement and the knowing/wisdom of the body, including the brain's motor cortex, which controls bodily motion.

MUSICAL/RHYTHMIC INTELLIGENCE
This intelligence is based on recognition of tonal patterns, including environmental sounds, and on sensitivity to rhythm and beats.

VERBAL/LINGUISTIC INTELLIGENCE
Related to written and spoken languages, this intelligence dominates most Western educational systems.

INTRAPERSONAL INTELLIGENCE
This intelligence relates to inner states of being, self-reflection, metacognition, and awareness of spiritual realities.

INTERPERSONAL INTELLIGENCE
This intelligence operates primarily through person-to-person relationships and communication.

Figure 11

PORTFOLIOS OF MULTIPLE INTELLIGENCES

COULD INCLUDE THE FOLLOWING ACTIVITIES AND ASSESSMENTS:

Figure 12

Verbal/ Linguistic	Logical/ Mathematical	Visual/Spatial	Bodily/ Kinesthetic	Musical/ Rhythmic	Interpersonal	Intrapersonal
• computer printouts	• puzzles	• artwork	• field trips	• background music in class	• group video, film, filmstrip	• problem-solving strategies
• tape recordings of readings	• problems solved on calculators	• photographs	• role playing	• songs for books, countries, people	• team computer programs	• goal setting
• reactions to guest speakers	• patterns and their relationships	• math manipulatives	• learning centers	• raps, jingles, cheers, poems	• think-pair-share	• reflective logs
• autobiographies	• lab experiments	• graphic organizers	• labs	• cooperative task trios	• divided journals	• divided journals
• biographies	• mathematical operations	• posters, charts, graphics, pictures	• outdoor education	• musical mnemonics	• metacognitive reflections	• metacognitive reflections
• mnemonics	• formulas/abstract symbols	• illustrations	• environmental studies	• choral reading	• independent reading times	• independent reading times
• reactions to films or videos	• analogies	• sketches	• sports/games	• tone pattern	• jigsaw	• silent reflection time
• scripts for radio shows	• time lines	• drawings	• cooperative learning	• wraparounds	• wraparounds	• concentration exercises
• captions for cartoons	• outlines	• paintings	• exercise breaks	• music and dance of different cultures	• electronic mail	• self-evaluation
• student-made bulletin boards	• Venn diagrams	• props for plays	• stretching	• musical symbols	• group songs, collages, poems	• visualization
• list of books read	• computer games	• demonstrations	• simulations		• class and group discussions	• self-discovery
• annotated bibliographies	• original word problems	• use of overhead or blackboard	• interviews		• rating scales	
	• mind maps	• storyboards	• projects		• group projects	
			• presentations		• group presentations	
			• dances			

* Many activities and assessments overlap into several intelligences.

Adapted from *If the Shoe Fits... How to Develop Multiple Intelligences in the Classroom* (Chapman, 1993)

Name ___Joe L.___ Grade ___4th___ Date ___Oct. 10___

THE SELECTION PROCESS USING A MULTIPLE INTELLIGENCE GRID
Unit: Space
Activities and Assessments for a Three-Week Unit

By using myriad ideas to incorporate the multiple intelligences, students have many choices about what they want to put in their portfolios. They can select one activity/assessment from each of the seven intelligences to include in their portfolio.

Logical/ Mathematical	Visual/Spatial	Verbal/ Linguistic	Interpersonal	Musical/ Rhythmic	Intrapersonal	Bodily/ Kinesthetic
• Graph the distances of planets from the sun or other planets	• Draw a picture of what you think a Martian looks like	• Develop a list of space vocabulary words	• Interview E.T. about his trip to earth	• Write a national anthem for one of the planets	• Meditate on being the first person to walk on the moon	• Act out man's first steps on the moon
• Calculate how long it would take to get to the moon traveling 100 miles per hour	• Make a model of the solar system	• Write a joke book for space creatures	• Role play the parts of each member of a space crew	• Write a planet rap song	• Describe how it would feel to be the first student in space	• Simulate the sun or the orbits of all the planets
• Classify planets by size and temperature	• Make a clay sculpture of one of the planets	• Write a short story set on a planet	• Plan a joint space expedition with Russia	• Create a new dance called the "Space Walk"	• Tell how you would feel if you did not see sunlight for a long time	• Create a sport that would be popular in space (no gravity)
		• Keep a diary about a trip you took in space	• Practice peer mediation	• Write poetry to the music from 2001 A Space Odyssey		

Student Comments (about selections): _____

I really liked all these assignments, but I chose the ones I think I did the best on. My planet rap song is my favorite.

Adapted from teachers, Cobb County, Georgia

Figure 13

Thematic Units or Projects—"Dream Theme"

Sometimes items are selected for a portfolio on the basis of a thematic unit. Instead of including items from the entire quarter or semester, the teacher and students focus the portfolio on a specific unit of study. The unit could range from two to five weeks in length and could include from five to ten items. If the class is studying Greek mythology for five weeks, it could choose to select entries that demonstrate each student's writing, reading, and speaking processes as well as their understanding of Greek myths, history, and customs.

For example, a thematic portfolio on mythology could include a poem about the first football game on Mt. Olympus, a modern version of the Twelve Labors of Hercules, a Venn diagram comparing the Greeks and the Trojans, a myth explaining the origin of fireflies, a video of Olympic events, and drawings of products derived from Greek names. (See sample portfolio in the conclusion, pages 139–154.)

How Are Entries Selected and Do They Meet Goals and Standards?

In conjunction with determining *what* goes into the portfolio, attention must be paid to *how* the entries are selected and whether or not they demonstrate a student's ability to meet criteria for quality work, learning outcomes or goals, and district, state, or national standards. Criteria and indicators for quality work can be established by the teacher and the students in the classroom. (See Chapter Seven.) In addition, the portfolio could be used to demonstrate accountability based upon instructional standards that have been developed by various organizations and state departments of education.

National Standards—"Think Globally"

During the past decade groups representing subject area professional associations, national accreditation organizations, and child advocacy organizations have done much work to create national standards. Each standard incorporates emergent knowledge in education as well as the best educational practices. Teachers often find these "national standards" to be an excellent source for determining local school or classroom standards and criteria for student achievement.

State Mandates—"High Stakes"

State standards currently being developed in many regions are also excellent sources for determining criteria to be used in selecting portfolio artifacts of important student achievement. In many

Criteria and indicators for quality work can be established by the teacher and the students in the classroom.

instances students and teachers together are able to translate standards in subject areas or learning processes into understandable criteria for performance. By using these criteria, teachers create student self-assessment forms and artifact selection forms. In this way the portfolio selection process assures that content, goals, and artifacts reflect clearly defined criteria that meet stated standards.

District Goals—"Act Locally"

Similarly, teachers who are required to implement district-mandated standards across the curriculum can develop criteria in key areas which will determine the selection of portfolio artifacts. When standards are translated into criteria and indicators of performance, they result in portfolios that reflect acceptable and outstanding levels of accomplishment at each level of student achievement.

Teacher/Student Created Criteria—"It's Up to Us!"

If the purpose of the portfolio is to be used in the classroom for students, teachers, and parents to review student work and to discuss during conferences, then the teacher and students should select entries that meet their own criteria. For example, the class could vote to include categories that make sure the portfolio contains representative work but at the same time gives students some choice as to which items they want to include. They can also create their own scoring devices to assess the items according to criteria and indicators.

Teachers who are required to implement district-mandated standards across the curriculum can develop criteria in key areas which will determine the selection of portfolio artifacts.

SELECTION CATEGORIES

Media	**Group Work**	**Individual Work**
cassettes	projects	papers
slides	performances	tests
videos	peer feedback	journals
pictures		logs
computer programs		
Processes	**Reflective**	**Multiple Intelligences**
biography of a work	self-assessments	logical/mathematical
rough drafts and	metacognitive	musical/rhythmic
final drafts	reflections	verbal/linguistic
sketches and final	statement of goals	bodily/kinesthetic
drawings	reflective journals	visual/spatial
attempts at problem-	artifact registry	interpersonal
solving/final		intrapersonal
solutions		

Figure 14

Who Will Select Items?

Who are the stakeholders in the portfolio process? Who will participate in the selection of artifacts? Once again, the answers must be based on the overriding purpose of the portfolio, but any combination of these may be involved in the process: state mandates, students, teachers, parents, and peers.

Mandated—"It's the Law"

If the portfolio is considered part of a formal assessment process to monitor student achievement and/or teacher accountability, the district or the state educational leaders will probably determine the pieces that should be selected. For example, a state might require the following—one biographical piece, a piece of creative writing, a résumé for a job, evidence of teamwork, an assignment that integrates two different subject areas, a problem and a solution, or a self-assessment of the student as a lifelong learner. Some state departments of education determine what pieces will be selected for "high-stakes" portfolios that often play a big role in the evaluation process.

Student-Selected Artifacts—"It's Up to Me!"

Some teachers choose to have students select all of the work they want to include in their portfolio. They recognize that students are the big stakeholders in the process and should become responsible for their own learning. Some students select only their best work; others include a few "works in progress," "unsatisfactory pieces," and "not yets." Others want to highlight their lives outside of school and choose to select extracurricular, hobby, job-related, or community projects that reveal the "whole" student. Wiggins (1994) stresses that the selection process should be thoughtful and fun—but also challenging.

Teacher-Selected Artifacts—"I Have Goals"

The teacher is obviously a critically important player in the selection of portfolio pieces. The teacher's input may be obvious or subtle. Often the teacher has to make the choices to ensure the items reflect school, district, or state requirements. These so-called "high-stakes" portfolios require certain entries. Other times the teacher has options to include any pieces that reflect the content or processes that are the key concepts in the course. Teachers may also want to mix student-generated work with her own observations, quarterly or semester progress reports, scores on important standardized tests or teacher-made tests, anecdotal records, absentee records, or other items that sometimes are included in the student's permanent

The teacher is obviously a critically important player in the selection of portfolio pieces.

record. In this case, the confidentiality of the portfolio is paramount. These types of entries limit the access of portfolios; peers and sometimes other teachers who might be involved in conferencing will not be able to review all the contents of the portfolios.

Teacher-Student Selected Artifacts—"Together Is Better"

Sometimes the teacher and student select artifacts that they both agree best meet standards and criteria. Teachers might plan for teacher-student selections to occur at natural intersections of teaching and learning—such as the completion of thematic units of study or at the end of the quarter. Often the teacher decides to include three or four items to meet her content goals or district goals and then allows students free choice on the rest of the selections. Another option would be for the teacher to ask students to include a writing assignment, but allow students to decide *which* writing assignment they will include.

Additionally, teachers can assign categories—creative writing pieces, group projects, artwork, performances, media projects, reflections, logs, journals, a self-check observation list—but allow students the freedom to look over their work and select their favorites. This allows the teacher to retain evidence of growth or achievement while permitting the student to retain his or her freedom of choice within the teacher's framework.

Peer-Selected Pieces—"All for One and One for All"

Peer-selected artifacts can be important pieces in student portfolios. Since students are intricately involved in the assessment process, they are capable of reviewing the work of other students, providing constructive feedback, and selecting pieces they feel should be included in another student's portfolio. For example, a student may feel a piece of artwork is not up to his usual standards and would rather not include it in his portfolio. A fellow student or the members of his group, however, recognize qualities in the piece that they feel would make it "worthy" of entry into the portfolio. They can ask the student to include the entry along with their commentary or reflection as to why they felt it should be included.

It is important that students involved in peer-selection have been trained in social skills so they know how to listen empathetically, can use encouraging words, know how to disagree with the idea (not the person), and know how to assess the quality of work on the basis of standards, criteria, and indicators discussed and, hopefully, developed

Peer-selected artifacts can be important pieces in student portfolios.

in class. The comments of a peer and the involvement of fellow students in the selection process of portfolios offer powerful evidence of the impact of team building, trust building, and cooperation in the development of a "community of learners" within the classroom.

Parents and Significant Others—"Tell Me What You Think"
It is important to try to include the parents and other significant persons (other teachers, counselors, brothers, sisters, principals, bus drivers) in the selection process. Students can take home entries and ask parents or others to select which ones to include in their portfolios. This procedure helps parents be a part of the learning process and allows students to legitimately discuss work and to value the opinions of other people—not just depend on the opinion of the teacher.

Often teachers provide parents with key questions to ask, guidelines, criteria, or pertinent information that will guide them in making their selection. The parents or significant others should then write a reflection piece stating what they liked about the entry and why they thought it should be included in the portfolio.

When Will These Items Be Selected?

This chapter has presented ideas for the teacher to consider in the *what*, *how*, and *who* aspects of the selection process. Another dimension to be considered is the *when*. Although there can be a wide variety of times at which students and teachers will complete the portfolio selection for conferences or exhibitions, there are five commonly used occasions to make final selections for the portfolio: parent conference dates; the end of a thematic unit; the end of quarters or semesters; the end of the year; and cumulative.

Parent Conferences—"Parent Talk"
The presentation of portfolios at parent conferences is a popular and valuable event in the lives of students, parents, and teachers. These conferences could take place during the end of any quarter or semester, or at the end-of-year evaluation time. The portfolio provides more concrete data than grades, checklists, or report cards for communicating learner outcomes, student achievements, and student goals and for discussing important concepts.

> The presentation of portfolios at parent conferences is a popular and valuable event in the lives of students, parents, and teachers.

End of Thematic Unit—"The End"

Whenever the class finishes a unit on a content topic, a book, a period of history, a learning process, or an integrated unit, they can share the artifacts they have collected.

End-of-Quarter/Semester Reports—"Seasons"

Portfolio selection and sharing aligns well with the traditional end-of-term reporting procedures that commonly occur in schools. When portfolios are reviewed on a quarterly or semester basis, students and parents have the opportunity to review previous goals and to fine-tune and reflect on work in progress. Teachers also have the opportunity to reflect on student progress, assemble anecdotal notes, and checklists, and assist students in making artifact selections that represent achievement of ongoing goals and learning processes.

End-of-Year—"It's a Wrap!"

The end of the year provides the final opportunity for students, teachers, parents, and others to select artifacts for the end-of-year portfolio that represents the key learning experiences and learning outcomes that students have achieved throughout the entire year. These portfolios can be shared during classroom or schoolwide exhibitions where parents, family, community members, and other educators are invited to browse through student portfolios and interview students about their learning. The selection of this final portfolio usually represents key learning, important concepts, "big questions," or thematic units, and other representative work from the whole year.

Cumulative—"Year-to-Year"

Some schools or districts decide to maintain cumulative portfolios that are passed on to each grade for several years or for the entire school period K–12. The cumulative portfolio can be designed to include satisfactory and exemplary student achievements of performance standards in important learning processes and subject areas throughout several years of each student's school career.

Either the teacher or the school can determine the checkpoints at which students will select or review portfolio contents to provide evidence of their achievements or to display the work that has been most significant to them as learners. Depending on the purposes of portfolios, the cumulative portfolio may be seen as an optimal format for reporting student achievement of school outcomes and standards. Periodically, a review and audit of the portfolio should take place to

> Portfolio selection and sharing aligns well with the traditional end-of-term reporting procedures that commonly occur in schools.

When items are selected for a portfolio depends on the purpose, the type, the school schedule, conference dates, and other logistics that make the whole portfolio process valuable as well as workable.

remove some items before adding new ones—otherwise no school could possibly store all the portfolios for such a long period. Another option for storage would be to keep each student's portfolio on a computer disk.

Therefore, *when* items are selected for a portfolio depends on the purpose, the type, the school schedule, conference dates, and other logistics that make the whole portfolio process valuable as well as workable. It is important to set the dates of check points throughout the year in order to assure regular monitoring and to allow time for review, reflection, self-assessment, and goal-setting.

"I kept saying, 'Maybe we should clean off the front of the refrigerator', but noooo..."

Examples: Select Key Artifacts

THE WHAT

PLANNING MATRIX: LEARNING-PROCESS PORTFOLIO

Curriculum

Assessment Tools	Speaking	Listening Attentively and Empathetically	Writing	Reading	Evaluating – Checking for Accuracy (Applying)	Reasoning	Problem Solving	Questioning/Predicting	Student Assessed
Journals	–	–	–	–	–	–	–	–	Yes
Audio or Video Samples	✓✓	✓	✓	✓✓	✓✓	✓	✓	✓✓	Yes
Teacher/Peer Checklist	✓✓	✓✓	✓	✓	✓✓	✓✓	✓✓	✓✓	Yes
Interviews	✓✓	✓✓	✓	✓	✓✓	✓	✓	✓	Yes
Extended Projects	✓	✓	✓	✓	✓	✓	✓	✓	Yes

✓ at least one artifact   ✓✓ two to five artifacts

✚ five to ten artifacts   – ongoing piece

THE HOW

Select items for the portfolio that meet state goals in science.

Goal	Portfolio Entry
Know basic vocabulary of biological science.	Vocabulary test
Know implications and limitations of technical development.	Book report on *Brave New World*
Know principles of scientific research.	Journal entry
Know processes of science.	Lab report on experiment

THE WHO

PARENT SELECTION

To: Parent/Significant Other

Please review the attached entries that may be included in _Jim R.'s_ portfolio and provide your feedback.

What piece most surprises you? Why?
The cartoon! I had no idea Jim could draw that well and think of such a clever caption.

Which piece do you feel needs more work? Why?
The job résumé. It makes me cringe when I see spelling and grammar errors.

Which piece do you want to include in the portfolio? Why?
The report on health care reform. Jim did a lot of research for that one.

Signature _Mr. John Ross_

THE WHEN

PORTFOLIO SCHEDULE FOR THE YEAR

October 5	Portfolio Review by Parents at Back-to-School Night
November 3	12-Week Review by: Peer / Teacher
February 5	12-Week Review by: Peer / Teacher / Students in Other Class
April 25	12-Week Review by: Parents/Significant Other / Cooperative Group Members / Teacher
June 5	Final Portfolio Review Teacher and Parents

TEACHER PLANNER
SELECTING KEY ARTIFACTS

I.   THE WHAT—What will be the curricular or learning areas for which student portfolios will be used?

[ ] Subject- or Content-Area Learning
[ ] Learning Processes
[ ] Multiple Intelligences
[ ] Combination Subject Area and Learning Processes
[ ] Thematic Units or Projects
[ ] Other

Comments:

_____

_____

II. THE HOW—Standards and Criteria for Portfolios

A. How will standards be determined?

B. What standards will be used?

[ ] National Standards
[ ] State Standards
[ ] Subject-Area Standards (Science, Mathematics, etc.)
[ ] Schoolwide or Districtwide Goals
[ ] Teacher/Student Created Criteria

Comments:

_____

_____

Blackline

(Teacher Planner Continued)

III. THE WHO—Who Will Participate in the Assessment Process and Selection of the Artifacts?

Choose	**Explain**
[ ] District- or State- Mandated	_____
[ ] Student-Selected	_____
[ ] Teacher-Selected	_____
[ ] Teacher/Student-Selected	_____
[ ] Peer-Selected	_____
[ ] Parent- and/or Others- Selected	_____

Comments:

_____

_____

IV. THE WHEN—When Will Work Be Selected for Inclusion in the Portfolio?

[ ] Parent Conferences   Date: _____
[ ] End of Thematic Unit   Date: _____
[ ] End of Quarter/Semester   Date: _____
[ ] End of Year   Date: _____
[ ] Cumulative (Year-to-Year) Years: _____

Comments:

_____

_____

©1994 by IRI/Skylight Publishing, Inc.

Blackline

MULTIPLE INTELLIGENCES PORTFOLIO

Name _____

Teachers and students brainstorm possible ideas for the portfolio and select one of each category to include in the portfolio.

Verbal/ Linguistic	Logical/ Mathematical	Visual/Spatial	Bodily/ Kinesthetic	Musical/ Rhythmic	Interpersonal	Intrapersonal

Blackline

CHAPTER 4:

INTERJECT
PERSONALITY

"Art is not a thing, it is a way."
—Elbert Hubbard (cited in Peter, 1977, p. 25)

INTERJECT PERSONALITY

Overview

After the key pieces are selected for inclusion in the portfolio, refinements need to be made. Just as artists interject their personality into their paintings with the style and technique of each brush stroke, so, too, students interject their personality into their portfolio.

Each portfolio is as unique as a fingerprint. No two portfolios look exactly alike, even if they contain the very same elements. The student tailors the look of the portfolio to present an intimate view of him- or herself. Personal choices and style, especially evident in the decorative covers, become the signature of the owner. Eisner (1993) makes the point, "We need to celebrate diversity and to cultivate the idiosyncratic aptitudes our students possess" (p. 23). Some portfolios will be signed off with a flourish of a fountain pen, while others will be neat and tidy. Some will be a riot of color and design, while others will be monochromatic and dignified. All reflect the personality of the owner.

Each portfolio is as unique as a fingerprint.

The portfolio appearance, design, and texture reflect the particular personality of the creator. That is exactly what makes portfolios valuable assessment tools! They allow a more intimate and holistic look at the person creating it. Some say, in fact, that the portfolio is a window into the personality, traits, skills, and talents of the person.

Introduction

"When who you are and what you do go to work, a powerful resource has arrived" (Dietz, 1992, p. 6).

The overall appearance of the portfolio is a reflection of its creator and owner. Although the essential ingredients are contained inside the portfolio, the attractiveness of the container and the *cover* are also of the utmost importance. You might argue, "You can't tell a book by its cover," but it's doubtful if you would pick up the book if the cover was not inviting.

The portfolio contains materials specially gathered and assembled to communicate a person's talents and achievements to others. Therefore, the more inviting the container, the more likely the viewer is to be initially drawn to the portfolio. The cover demonstrates the student's pride in his or her work. According to Glasser (1986), this is how students learn to become critical of the quality of their work.

Options for decorating the cover are innumerable, but color, design, graphics, and texture depend somewhat on the size, shape, and composition of the container. Decisions about design are explored later in this chapter.

Students can also interject their personality into the portfolio in the *organization* of the portfolio. Although this is fully explored in the chapter on collecting and organizing, the page layout is dependent on the organization of the contents. Many facets of the *page layout* warrant attention: number and size of items on a page; ways to connect items and highlight particular artifacts; innovative ways to include odd-sized or unusual items.

The student's personality jumps off the page through the *tone* or *mood* evidenced in the portfolio. Tone or mood may be subtle, but both convey important information about the creator. For example, students who have a good sense of humor may want to reflect it by using cartoons, riddles, or humorous sketches in their portfolios.

The student's personality jumps off the page through the *tone* or *mood* evidenced in the portfolio.

The opportunity for creativity in portfolio design is endless, but the key is to fashion the portfolio so that it is a complimentary representation of its creator. How creating portfolios affect and impact the student creators is evidenced in these testimonials (cited in Bower, 1994, p. 3):

"A portfolio is a reflection of me . . ." —Emelyne

"Personal feelings and opinions are also included in the portfolio." —Jamil

"Most of all this portfolio gives me the chance to express myself about what I really think about this math course." —Will

Ideas

Cover

Gather Items—"Collage"

Personal collages may be created for the cover. Students can gather pictures or materials that reflect something about themselves. Once they have gathered a number of items, they can arrange them in a collage on the cover of their portfolio. Collages are time-consuming to design, but students may gain many insights as they create the collage design.

Personal Photos—"Photo Album"

A photograph of the student on the portfolio cover adds a personal touch. This cover is especially useful if the portfolio follows students from grade to grade, because it records the student's physical development as well as his or her intellectual development.

Designs—"Pattern Design"

Another option is for students to be as creative as possible and develop cover designs that are totally unique. The portfolio's cover can be as special as its contents. The outside of the portfolio, after all, invites the reader to look further and to explore what's inside.

Organization

The overall organization of the portfolio may be predetermined by the teacher or it may be left up to the student. Please refer to Chapter Two for more information about options for storage, organizational flow, and organizational tools.

Page Layout

Messing Around—"Gallery"

The portfolio may be contained in various ways, but most of the works will be kept on pages. Artists arrange their portfolio pages artfully. Students can do the same. Page layout is critical to the presentation. Usually, students arrange the artifacts on the page in the most artful or creative way possible.

Simple Design—"Geo-Metrics"

Some students may prefer a geometric layout, or a simple design for each page. These designs tend to highlight one piece and provide a fairly straightforward look-through for the viewer.

A photograph of the student on the portfolio cover adds a personal touch.

Groupings—"Clutter and Cluster"

Students may prefer to group their artifacts to suggest quantity and quality by placing more than one artifact on a page. This style of page composition requires a little more time to assemble, but it provides a rich portfolio of work since more items are displayed.

Connectors—"Abstract Threads"

Students may enhance their page design with abstract graphics or decorative designs throughout the portfolio. These may be drawn in ink or marker, or may be made from materials such as yarn, stickers, or dots.

Mood or Tone
Mood—"Attention"

Some may feel that the mood or tone is obscure and too difficult to assess or include in the portfolio. But, if a teacher wishes to emphasize the metacognitive reflection of the student, every design detail is justified. As students develop their portfolios, decisions made about selectivity, design, refinements, and presentation are reflected in the final product. By calling students' attention to the concept of mood, students will be more aware of the subtle messages that their portfolio gives to others.

Tone—"Target Tone"

Students can ensure that they achieve the appropriate mood or tone (academic, aesthetic, serious, humorous, competent) by targeting the audience. The student should ask him- or herself: What traits and characteristics am I looking for? Once the target audience is clear, certain things can be added or highlighted to give the desired effect.

As students develop their portfolios, decisions made about selectivity, design, refinements, and presentation are reflected in the final product.

Examples: Interject Personality

COVERS

Personal Collage

Patterned Design

Photo Album Cover

Textured Design

ORGANIZATION

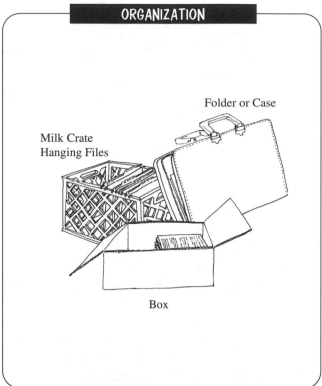

Folder or Case

Milk Crate Hanging Files

Box

PAGE LAYOUT

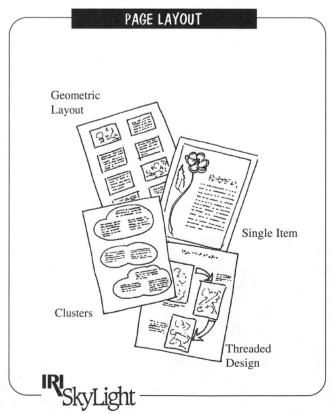

Geometric Layout

Single Item

Clusters

Threaded Design

MOOD/TONE

Busy

Sedate

IRI SkyLight

TEACHER PLANNER

1.　**Draw Some Ideas for a Cover Design:**

2.　**Jot Down Organizational Ideas:**

3.　**Sketch a Possible Page Layout:**

4.　**Make Memos on Mood and Tone:**

Blackline

PAGE LAYOUT

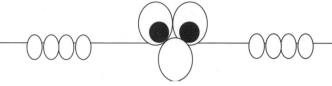

How will it look?

1. Number of Items _____

2. Size of Items _____

3. Color/Black & White _____

4. Cluster Design _____

5. Linear Design _____

6. Thread Connecting Items _____

7. Overlapped Items/Separated Items _____

8. Other _____

©1994 by IRI/Skylight Publishing, Inc.

Blackline

CHAPTER 5:

REFLECT METACOGNITIVELY

"No art was ever less spontaneous than mine.
What I do is the result of reflection and study."
—Edgar Degas (cited in Peter, 1977, p. 31)

REFLECT METACOGNITIVELY

Overview

A tiny light mounted on the frame of a picture reveals the subtle details of the portrait. The subtle details of student portfolios are revealed as students reflect on selected works. Each piece included in the portfolio needs several "metacognitive moments" when students plan, monitor, and evaluate the value of the artifact, both as an individual piece and in relation to the whole portfolio (Belanoff & Dickson, 1991).

One relatively easy way to reflect on portfolio pieces is to tag or label each piece. The label or tag explains the value of the piece and why the piece has particular significance in the collection (Mills-Courts & Amiran, 1991). These tag lines, labels, comments, and points provide a "running monologue." This monologue brings the portfolio alive for the viewer who has not taken part in the development of the portfolio or who has not had an opportunity to discuss the portfolio with its creator.

Reflection also engages the student in metacognition. As students move in and out of reflection, they survey the overall schemata for their portfolio. They also automatically shift into a monitoring mode when each additional artifact is weighed against the whole portfolio. And, of course, students naturally evaluate as they reflect about just why the piece is valued and should be included in the finished portfolio (Burke, 1992).

The intrinsic value of the portfolio strategy lies in the opportunity for metacognitive reflection by students.

Introduction

The best research on cognitive development suggests that it is extremely important for students to think about their own thinking, and reflect on how they learn and why they fail to learn (Mills-Courts & Amiran, 1991). When someone uses metacognition they can "describe the steps and sequences, used before, during, and after problem solving" (Costa, 1991, p. 23).

The creation of portfolios as viable assessment tools is, in itself, a marked improvement in evaluation methodology. However, the intrinsic value of the portfolio strategy lies in the opportunity for metacognitive reflection by students as they plan, monitor, and evaluate themselves throughout the entire process and as they uncover the reasons why things have been included in the portfolio.

The portfolio is a wonderful decision-making tool for the student (Mills-Courts & Amiran, 1991). It not only fosters organizational skills as students devise a system for collecting artifacts in a regular and systematic way, but also fosters higher-order tasks, such as predicting, prioritizing, and ranking. Portfolio development is an ongoing process that provides ample opportunity for student-directed and student-initiated problem solving.

In this chapter, ideas for metacognitive reflection are explored: in the planning stages, as students think ahead about the portfolio content and design; in the monitoring stages, as students pay careful attention to details as the portfolio takes on a shape of its own; and in the evaluation stages, as students critically assess their work to ensure quality and accountability. Within these three major categories a number of ideas are suggested. Some are quite obvious and easy to implement, while others are more abstract and require more thoughtful reflection. No matter what metacognitive strategies are used, they are sure to enhance the overall portfolio and give students beneficial personal insights.

Ideas

Planning Stage
Visualization—"Film Footage"
One of the most powerful techniques for personal reflective planning is the ability to envision the desired goal or outcome (Fogarty & Bellanca, 1989). Students can visualize a favorable reception of their artifacts by others. When students form this scenario in the mind's eye, they can shape their work to achieve that end. To help students become more skillful at visualizing completed and pleasing work to include in their portfolios, teachers can have students practice recalling things and "running" through them in their minds. For example, students might try to visualize their bedrooms or the ketchup bottle in the refrigerator.

Then, students can practice imaging things that are not stored in their memories but must be created in the mind, such as a dream car. Finally, students can think about a particular assignment and try to picture it in its final form. An essay, a charcoal sketch, or a class report are all examples of work that might be visualized in the planning stages.

No matter what metacognitive strategies are used, they are sure to enhance the overall portfolio and give students beneficial personal insights.

Strategic Planning—"Road Map"

A mental road map can be used to plot the "route" or process before embarking on a trip (Fogarty, 1994). This helps students clarify their goals for each piece included in the portfolio. Naturally, this plan is embedded in the earliest steps of the portfolio development that are discussed fully in Chapter Three. However, just as with any dynamic process, as the portfolio begins to take shape, it may not appear as the student originally envisioned. Therefore, the student may have to adjust and revise the strategic plan on occasion.

Establish Benchmarks—"Checking"

A strategic plan implies the existence of clearly defined benchmarks along the way (Burke, 1993). Portfolio development is a long-term project. And, as with any extensive undertaking, it is often best to lay out the plan in manageable chunks. By "chunking" the project and establishing benchmarks, success is ensured. This "chunking" is similar to what is used with research projects and lab reports, as well as portfolio development. Benchmarks may be established for collecting, selecting, and reflecting on the portfolio.

A strategic plan implies the existence of clearly defined benchmarks along the way.

"MY TEACHER SAID I'M RIDING ALONG IN A 'NO PASSING' ZONE!"

© Vanselow Reprinted with permission.

Monitoring Stage
Labeling—"Soup Cans"

As students gather and compile items, they employ metacognition. As each item is scrutinized, an "inner voice" directs the activity, providing reflective comments about why a particular piece is valued. Labeling is a strategy that directs students to listen to that "inner voice" (Fogarty, 1994). Labels can include a key phrase or comment that is placed either on or next to the artifact. Labels might include: Awesome! A First Draft! Hardest Math Problem I've Ever Done. My Teacher Liked This One! Final Report! and Log Entry I Had Forgotten. This initial labeling provides a quick inventory of what is included in the collection and gives insight about what is valued.

Labels can include a key phrase or comment that is placed either on or next to the artifact.

Figure 15

Questions to Ask—"Bridging"

Asking key questions is a viable reflective technique for bridging ideas from one situation to another. For example, as students contemplate the various decisions about their portfolios, questions may help them clarify their purposes, selections, and presentation concerns. Students can ask themselves *how* and *why* questions to monitor their decisions: Why am I including this? How might I present this briefly, yet effectively? Why would this be essential? How can I eliminate some of these artifacts and still present a complete picture? Exactly what am I trying to convey? This self-questioning helps students become more aware and explicit about the selection process. The questions help students bridge the various elements together into a more holistic look at the entire portfolio.

Evaluating Stage

Artifact Registry—"Log-a-Line"
Perhaps one of the easiest and most helpful metacognitive strategies is the portfolio registry (Dietz, 1992). The registry provides an anecdotal record or biography of the work over time. As the student adds or deletes items from the portfolio, he or she may make a memo in the registry. This memo might include name, date, and reason for including or excluding the artifact. If the registries are kept up to date, the history of the portfolio is readily available for anyone to see.

Anecdotes—"Story Time"
Learning is embedded in stories and vignettes students tell. As students relay the stories behind the artifacts, learning comes alive for the listeners and for the speakers. Student pairs may take turns telling stories about the creation of their artifacts and this sharing can become a part of the portfolio development. At regular intervals, as students add things to their portfolios, students may be asked to share the anecdote with one other student. Appropriate story starters might include the following list by Jalongo (1992). (See Figure 16.)

> **As students relay the stories behind the artifacts, learning comes alive for the listeners and for the speakers.**

STARTERS

The metaphor . . .	One insight . . .
At least . . .	A reflection . . .
Compare to . . .	This symbolizes . . .
Looking back . . .	I assessed them . . .
The change I made . . .	One choice . . .

Figure 16

Examples: Reflect Metacognitively

PLANNING

Strategic Plan

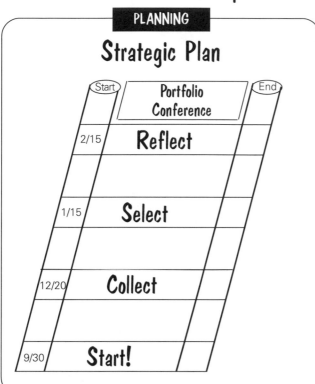

	Portfolio Conference	
Start		End
2/15	**Reflect**	
1/15	**Select**	
12/20	**Collect**	
9/30	**Start!**	

MONITORING

Labeling

Post-it Note

Sticker Label

Border Label

EVALUATE

Bridging

Now I ask myself...

1. Why am I including this?

2. Is this essential to my goal?

3. How might I connect this to what comes before? after?

EVALUATE

Registry

In	Out	Artifact	Comment
4/28	5/12	Puppet	It's a great project to tell about
5/12		Videotape	Tape of puppet show is easier to store and show
5/20	6/5	Letter to Agency	Summarizes my goals
6/2		The Crimson (School Newspaper)	My article on graffiti is in it
6/5		New Letter	Update the other one

TEACHER PLANNER

Choose your metacognitive strategies and describe how you will use them. Select one from each major area—planning, monitoring, and evaluating.

PLANNING:

Visualization Exercise:

Strategic Plan Activity:

Establishing Benchmarks:

MONITORING:

Labeling Strategy:

Bridging Questions:

EVALUATING:

Artifact Registry Refinement:

Anecdotes:

©1994 by IRI/Skylight Publishing, Inc.

PORTFOLIO CONFERENCE

Date _____

Start   **END HERE**   End

RESPECT
(Share yourself through exhibitions.)

Date   Date

PERFECT
(Refine, Revise)

Date   Date

REFLECT
(Why are they important?)

Date   Date

SELECT
(Seven to Ten Items)

Date   Date

COLLECT
(Everything)

Date   **START HERE**   Date

IRI SkyLight

Blackline

©1994 by IRI/Skylight Publishing, Inc.

REFLECTIVE STEMS FOR INDIVIDUAL PIECES IN THE PORTFOLIO

This is my favorite piece because…

I'll remember this piece 20 years from now because…

If I could do this piece over again, I would…

This piece will surprise many people because…

My parent(s) liked this piece because…

This piece was my greatest challenge because…

Write your own stems:

SAMPLE BRIDGING QUESTIONS

Directions: Select some of these "bridging questions" or write your own to help you reflect on items in your portfolio.

1. Why have I chosen this piece?

2. What are its strengths? weaknesses?

3. Why is it important?

4. How/where does it fit in with what I already know?

5. What category does it fit into?

6. How might I label it appropriately?

7. What if I took it out of my portfolio?

8. How do I think others will react to it?

9. On a scale of 1-10, I give it a _____ because _____.

10. Others:

Blackline

NOTES:

_____
_____
_____
_____
_____
_____
_____
_____
_____
_____
_____
_____
_____
_____
_____
_____
_____
_____
_____
_____
_____
_____
_____

CHAPTER 6:

INSPECT TO SELF-ASSESS

*"A man paints with his brains,
not with his hands."*
—Michelangelo (cited in Peter, 1977, p. 31)

INSPECT TO SELF-ASSESS

Overview

In contrast to the piece-by-piece reflection phase, the inspect phase overviews the entire collection of works and the insights it reveals to students. In this phase students review their short- and long-term goals while checking how the portfolio adheres to those goals.

Just as artists must at some point review their entire body of work, so students must review their collection of artifacts. Students can use this time to match their output with predetermined goals, review their overall strengths and weaknesses, and evaluate future directions or make necessary adjustments.

The inspecting phase is the time for an informal self-evaluation, a check of the overall direction desired by the student. It is the opportunity to ask questions about the next steps along the "chosen" or "changing" pathways. It's the moment of truth that signals to learners whether or not they are on track and what measures they might need to take to realign their aims and goals or to set new goals that may lead them in an entirely different direction.

The inspecting phase is the time for an informal self-evaluation, a check of the overall direction desired by the student.

Frog school pictures

Introduction

"When teachers invite students to become partners in inquiry, to collaborate with them in wondering about what and how students are learning, schools become more thoughtful places" (Atwell, 1991, p. 3).

An exciting outcome of using portfolios is the recognition by students that *they* themselves have become the center of the learning process. This occurs when teachers develop thoughtful outcomes for their students and get them to think about their learning achievements. Students who are active participants in the portfolio collection and selection process are empowered to become autonomous, independent thinkers, problem solvers, and creators of new knowledge.

When teachers invite, extend, and commend the learning of their students, teachers move more closely toward genuine assessment. In fact, they approach the root meaning of assess—"assidere"—which means "to sit beside." Learning comes to be "seen as a joint venture where students and teachers learn together. It then follows that the responsibility for evaluation must also be shared by the teacher and the students (Howell & Woodley, cited in Goodman, Bird, & Goodman, 1992, p. 87).

Wiggins (1994) says the aim of educators "should be to make all students able to monitor and reflect on their own work so they can self-adjust" as needed. Students need to take responsibility for inspecting their own work for quality. They should not depend on a teacher to follow them around throughout life giving them stickers, happy faces, or A's and B's. Too many students become dependent upon authority figures with red pens to provide feedback on how they are doing.

As people go through life, they have to *inspect* their own products or performances according to standards, self-assess, self-adjust, and set new goals on an ongoing basis. Student autonomy has become an emergent goal of education, because "autonomy in the intellectual realm means ability to govern oneself by being able to take relevant factors into account" (Kamii, Clark, & Dominick, 1994, p. 675)

An exciting outcome of using portfolios is the recognition by students that *they* themselves have become the center of the learning process.

Through the portfolio inspection and self-assessment process, student autonomy is "constructed by each [student] through the consideration of other persons' points of view and rights, not just his or her own" (Glazer, 1993, p. 107).

Goal setting and self-inspection also foster self-initiative. Students become willing to take intellectual risks and to assume both responsibility and accountability for their learning.

Ideas

To promote student autonomy, initiative, self-assessment, and goal setting, teachers may choose from a palette of assessment tools such as checklists, logs, journals, learning lists, stem statements, and rubrics. Tools can be used to include students in evaluating group and individual works, performances, or entire products. These assessment tools are most effective when they assist students in achieving ownership and responsibility or a sense of "voice" in determining the direction of their authentic learning and how their journey will be accomplished.

Getting Started

Two ideas are presented here to get started. One is establishing criteria and the other is using checklists with students.

Establishing Criteria—"What's Important"

In the reflective stage, students look at each *individual piece* in their portfolio and react to it. In the inspection stage, students look at the *whole portfolio* and reflect on how well the entries show whether they have met the criteria for quality work. The teacher and students might list criteria they think are important for meeting goals, outcomes, or local and state standards.

For example, criteria for a finished portfolio might include several of the following: evidence of thoughtfulness, growth and development, process, understanding, and cooperation. (See Figure 17 for other possible criteria.)

In the inspection stage, students look at the *whole portfolio* and reflect on how well the entries show whether they have met the criteria for quality work.

CRITERIA FOR PORTFOLIOS

Accuracy of Information
Completeness
Connections to Other Subjects
Correctness of Form
Creativity
Development of Process
Diversity of Entries
Diversity of Multiple Intelligences
Evidence of Thoughtfulness
Growth and Development

Insightfulness
Knowledge of Concepts
Organization
Persistence
Progress
Quality Products
Self-Assessment
Visual Appeal

Figure 17

Obviously, teachers and students need to prioritize which criteria are the most important and focus on them. Later, the list could be expanded as students become more proficient in the portfolio process, or as some criteria are introduced.

Chapter Seven (p. 90, 91, and 93) gives examples of how these criteria can be expanded to include specific indicators or characteristics as well as how a scoring sheet or rubric can be developed to provide more specific feedback and/or evaluate the portfolio for a grade. Even if the portfolio is not graded, however, students still need to examine their work using the criteria since this process leads to a more thoughtful inspection of their work.

Checklists—"Checking It Twice"
Even though checklists are often used only for observational and anecdotal assessment, they can assist students in self-assessment and peer-assessment. Students can evaluate their progress in developing work habits, study skills, and organizational abilities. They can also become engaged in reflecting on "intelligent behaviors" such as persistence, checking for accuracy, and insightfulness (Costa, 1991).

Checklists can assist students in self-assessment and peer-assessment.

SELF-ASSESSMENT CHECKLIST

Student: _____ BOB _____   Date: _____ 10/12 _____

Criterion—"Persistence"	Frequently	Sometimes	Seldom	Not Yet
Indicators:				
1. I know how to access information.	✓			
2. I try several approaches.		✓		
3. I do not give up quickly.		✓		
4. I have patience.				✓
5. I brainstorm alternative solutions.	✓			
6. I check my own work.		✓		
7. I write several drafts.		✓		

Figure 18

If students need to learn how to become self-regulating, they need to monitor their own behavior, work habits, thinking skills, and the behavior and processes of their peers.

Teachers sometimes feel that *they* are the only ones that can observe students and use checklists. If students need to learn how to become self-regulating, they need to monitor their own behavior, work habits, thinking skills, and the behavior and processes of their peers. Moreover, these checklists provide concrete information (dates, incidents, scoring) that can be used during conferences and when students set their new goals. Another example of a student self-assessment checklist is on page 80.

Students can review their group behavior by checking off the times they or their peers demonstrate positive social skills. They can then review the checklist and reflect on how well they have done or what they still need to do to improve. Therefore, teachers, students, and groups can all use checklists to inspect learning skills, social skills, or behaviors.

Goal Setting

Once students begin to self-monitor with checklists, it's time to guide them into some personal goal setting. Logs and journals are the most appropriate for this early stage of student goal setting and subsequent self-inspection to see if they are on track.

Learning Logs—"Log Your Reflections"

Learning logs promote student self-reflection and goal setting. "Logs usually consist of short, more objective entries that contain mathematics, problem-solving entries, observations of science experiments, questions about the lecture or reading, lists of outside readings, homework assignments, or anything that lends itself to keeping records" (Burke, 1993, p. 84). Daily learning logs enable students to take ownership of their learning goals and outcomes. Students set their own learning goals and monitor their individual progress toward these goals. Learning logs can also include artifacts that prove that the student has achieved certain goals. Visovatti calls these logs "proof I'm a reader" (Visovatti, 1994, p. 13).

Reflective Journals—"Mirror, Mirror . . ."

Reflective journals engage students in ongoing goal setting and reflections and foster the development of interpersonal skills. Unlike logs which are momentary pauses in the learning process, journals provide students with an ongoing diary of their daily responses, their subjective feelings, or a narrative viewpoint. Goals set by students are continuously monitored and reflected upon through the use of this journal.

Double-Entry Journals—"Double Dip"

Double-entry journals enable students to record experiences in one column and to respond to or reflect on these experiences in a second column. This format helps students formulate initial observations about a subject in one column and then wait until they have learned more about the topic (through time, coursework, readings, videos) before they write in the second column, "upon reflection." Students are able to see how they often change their feelings based upon new experiences. When used to inspect portfolios, students can write about their initial feelings about preparing a portfolio and then reflect many weeks later after they complete their portfolio. (An example is on page 80.)

Dialogue Journals—"He Said, She Said"

Dialogue journals can take the form of learning logs, reflective journals, or double-entry journals. But dialogue journals are also read by the teacher or others. Dialogue journals promote the development of a student's "voice." They also allow the teacher to enter into the metacognitive reflection process with each learner. Teachers can write responses directly into the student journal or attach brief notes to the student. The dialogue journals can be used throughout the portfolio or saved until the whole portfolio is ready to be inspected. The feedback the other person provides may raise new questions, validate what the student feels, or offer suggestions to expand on ideas or entries. Constructive feedback is critical to the portfolio process.

Learning Lists—"First, Second, Third . . ."

Learning lists are very similar to learning logs, but are used in cooperation with other learners or between the student and the teacher. Learning lists include stem statements that start students thinking about specific attributes or objectives within the learning process. Learning lists are tools that enable them to "think backward" about their achievements, acknowledge or celebrate them, and record them in a sequential way.

Many teachers interview each student about revisions or additions to learning lists. Various stem statements are created for lists of things students have learned to get them thinking about "New things I have learned," "One thing I'm having trouble with," or "Stories I have written."

Pictorial Lists—"Draw-a-Long"

Pictorial lists are an adaptation of learning lists. Younger children can use the pictorial list to draw pictures. Older students can use a class camera to capture moments of learning that they value, attach pictures to a response sheet, and write their reasons for valuing the activity (Burke, 1991).

Analyzing Strengths and Areas of Concern—"Have and Have Nots"

If students are to develop the critical thinking skills of analysis, synthesis, and evaluation, they need to review their own work and analyze their strengths and their areas of concern or "not yet" areas. It is important that students analyze their attributes through several lenses: content, processes, and social skills. Well-rounded students

Learning lists include stem statements that start students thinking about specific attributes or objectives within the learning process.

demonstrate competence in all areas and are aware of areas that need improvement. The following example shows one option:

MY STRENGTHS AND PROBLEM AREAS
SOCIAL STUDIES

Name : _Jeff B._   Grade:_7_

My Strengths	Content/ Subject Matter	I loved studying about Egypt and I read three books on the pyramids. I feel like an expert.
	Processes (writing, reading, thinking, etc.)	I really like to read—some of the books I select are high-school level but I have no problems with them. I also write creative stories.
	Social Skills (cooperation, behavior)	I am a good organizer in the groups and I always listen to others. Other group members respect my work.
My Problem Areas	Content/ Subject Matter	I receive low grades on research reports because I use only a few sources. I also tend to "copy" too much.
	Processes (writing, reading, thinking, etc.)	I can't spell anything. I proofread, but I can't look up _every_ word. I'm a creative writer who can't cope with form.
	Social Skills (cooperation, behavior)	Sometimes I get impatient with my group. It takes too long for them to decide what to do—I'd rather do it myself sometimes because I can do a better job.

Signed: _Jeff B._

Figure 19

Well-rounded students demonstrate competence in all areas and are aware of areas that need improvement.

Setting Short- and Long-Term Goals—"Goal Setting"
After students reflect and inspect their portfolio, it is time to analyze, evaluate, and make some plans. Goal setting is a crucial step in portfolio development because it forces students to monitor and reflect on their current learning and self-adjust as needed for future learning. The autonomous student needs to take the initiative so he can progress to checkpoint goals he sets for himself. Often students find it more manageable to break goals into two categories—short-term and long-term.

Goal setting is a crucial step in portfolio development because it forces students to monitor and reflect on their current learning and self-adjust as needed for future learning.

GOAL-SETTING SHEET

Student: _____Jeff B._____ Quarter: __1st__

Subject: __Social Studies–7th Grade__ Date: __Oct. 20__

Short-Term Goals	Target Date
1. Learn how to use spell check.	Nov. 20
2. Use more graphics in portfolio.	Dec. 20
3. Work on my grammar—subject-verb agreement, verb tense	Feb. 3

Long-Term Goals	Target Date
1. Complete long-term projects on time.	May 25
2. Talk more slowly and articulate.	May 25
3. Have more patience with my group members and offer to help them.	May 25

Date of Next Conference: _____Feb. 3_____

Figure 20

Short-term goals can usually be met by the date of the next portfolio conference. Often these goals are critical elements in portfolio conferences because teachers and students discuss whether the student has not met, has met, or has exceeded his or her goals from the last portfolio conference. Students then have to reflect on why they think they didn't meet their goals or find out what help they need and from whom to accomplish the goals. If they meet the goals they can then set new ones. The process is ongoing since students have to constantly assess and reassess where they have been, where they are, and, most importantly, where they are going.

It is important that the goals are not solely academic goals. Sometimes responsibility and interpersonal skills are equally important and necessary for students to succeed. Moreover, if students cannot seem to meet their own goals, they may need to develop a specific action plan and/or enlist the help of peers, counselors, parents, or teachers to help them meet their goals within a specific time frame.

The inspection phase of portfolio development enhances the reflection and metacognition developed in earlier chapters. It also allows students to play a vital role in their learning and to "change the course" of their goals as they explore new directions, review their overall strengths and weaknesses, and evaluate future pathways.

Final Decisions

Strategies for getting started and for the initial stages of student goal setting are followed by some final decisions about how the student sees things going. Am I meeting the established criteria? Am I meeting my personal goals—both long-term and short-term? How do I self-inspect? How do I know I'm on track?

Reviewing Criteria and Self-Assessing—"How Am I?"

Students can informally assess their own work based upon the criteria established as well as their reflections on individual pieces and their inspection of the whole portfolio. By reviewing the standards and criteria, students can make an informed decision about how they have fulfilled their own goals. A more formal assessment can be made using a scoring rubric that measures specific indicators under each score. (See Chapter 7, pages 90, 91, and 93.) But students are still capable of reviewing their own work and "adjusting" as needed before they begin revising their portfolios or begin a new one. They can analyze their own strengths and areas of concern and then set short-term and long-term goals to enhance their strengths and to improve their areas of concern.

Students can informally assess their own work based upon the criteria established as well as their reflections on individual pieces and their inspection of the whole portfolio.

Examples: Inspect to Self-Assess

GETTING STARTED

Self-Assessment Checklist

☑ Self   ☐ Peer   ☐ Teacher

Student: Jeff   Date: April 11, 1994

	Frequently	Sometimes	Not Yet
WORK HABITS:			
• Gets work done on time	✓	–	–
• Asks for help when needed	–	✓	–
• Takes initiative	–	✓	–

Comments: *It's hard getting used to asking the group and teachers to help, but I'm getting better.*

	Frequently	Sometimes	Not Yet
STUDY SKILLS:			
• Organizes work	✓	–	–
• Takes good notes	✓	–	–
• Uses time well	✓	–	–

Comments: *Since our base group has made this a goal, and we worked outside of class, I really am doing much better at this.*

	Frequently	Sometimes	Not Yet
SOCIAL SKILLS:			
• Works well with others	✓	–	–
• Listens to others	✓	–	–
• Helps others	✓	–	–

Comments: *My group is great. We have really done good work on all our assignments. I've learned how to listen and help. My group has really helped me.*

Signed: Jeff B.

(Adapted from Burke, 1993)

GOAL SETTING

Double-Entry Journal

Student Name: Jeff   Grade: 7
Date: 9/1   Subject: Social Studies   Date: 11/3

Starting My Portfolio	Finishing My Portfolio
Oh no! Another notebook to keep. I always manage to lose it before the end of the quarter. This time we have to show it to *other* people besides the teacher. I don't know how to type and I can't do artwork. I'm in big trouble!	I can't believe how hard I worked on this thing. I learned word processing because everyone else was typing theirs. I am pretty proud. Some of my friends read it and really liked it. My mom will love it. She'll probably show it to all the relatives.

FINAL DECISIONS

Analysis of My Strengths and Weaknesses

Old Me (Weaknesses): wrote one draft, never proofread, never showed work to others, used verbal intelligence, never gave a thought to learning

New Me (Strengths): write 3 drafts, use spell check, have peers read everything, use all seven intelligences, reflect on my own thinking

I still need improvement in:
- grammar
- artwork
- neatness
- talking too much in groups
- paraphrasing

Signed: Jeff B.

FINAL DECISIONS

Goal Setting

Short-term (3 months)
1. Learn how to use grammar check on computer.
2. Include at least 10 books in bibliography.
3. Learn how to use video camera for group performances.
4. Work on my intrapersonal intelligence.

Jeff's Goals

Long-term (6 months)
1. Be more creative.
2. Take an art class as an elective.
3. Have someone in group tutor me in grammar.
4. Work on not interrupting others.

Target Date: 11/3 (next portfolio conference)
Target Date: 5/8 (final portfolio conference)

Comments: *I've decided I need to learn everything I can about technology (videos, computers) to succeed.*

Signed: Jeff   Date: 11/5

IRI SkyLight

TEACHER PLANNER

Getting Started

Establish Criteria: _____
_____

Checklists: _____
_____

Goal Setting

Logs: _____
_____

Journals: _____
_____

Learning Lists: _____
_____

Final Decision

Self-Inspection: _____
_____

Analysis of Strengths and Areas of Concern: _____
_____

Goal Setting: _____
_____

Blackline

SELF-ASSESSMENT CHECKLIST

Directions: Select criteria to observe and list specific indicators that describe those criteria. (See example, p. 80.)

Student: _____ **Class:** _____

Portfolio Conference Date: _____

☐ **Teacher Date** _____ **Signed** _____

☐ **Peer   Date** _____ **Signed** _____

☐ **Self   Date** _____ **Signed** _____

	Frequently	Sometimes	Not Yet
_____			
• _____	_____	_____	_____
• _____	_____	_____	_____
• _____	_____	_____	_____
• _____	_____	_____	_____
_____			
• _____	_____	_____	_____
• _____	_____	_____	_____
• _____	_____	_____	_____
• _____	_____	_____	_____
_____			
• _____	_____	_____	_____
• _____	_____	_____	_____
• _____	_____	_____	_____
• _____	_____	_____	_____
_____			
• _____	_____	_____	_____
• _____	_____	_____	_____
• _____	_____	_____	_____
• _____	_____	_____	_____

COMMENTS: _____
_____

IRI SkyLight

Blackline

DOUBLE-ENTRY JOURNAL

Student: _____ Grade: _____

Subject: _____ Date: _____

Starting My Portfolio	Upon Completion of My Portfolio

IRI
SkyLight
Blackline

MY STRENGTHS AND WEAKNESSES

Old Me
(Weaknesses)

New Me
(Strengths)

I still need improvement in:

Signed: _____ Date: _____

IRI SkyLight

©1994 by IRI/Skylight Publishing, Inc.

Blackline

GOAL SETTING

Short-Term   **Long-Term**

1. _____   1. _____

2. _____   2. _____

name or picture

3. _____   3. _____

4. _____   4. _____

Target Date: _____   Target Date: _____
(next portfolio conference)   (final portfolio conference)

Comments: _____

_____

Signed: _____   Date: _____

NOTES:

_____

_____

_____

_____

_____

_____

_____

_____

_____

_____

_____

_____

_____

_____

_____

_____

_____

_____

_____

_____

_____

_____

_____

CHAPTER 7:

PERFECT AND EVALUATE

"An artist never really finishes his work;
he merely abandons it."
—Paul Valero (cited in Peter, 1977, p. 26)

PERFECT AND EVALUATE

Overview

In preparation for the portfolio conference with parents, both the student and teacher may want to perfect the portfolio by adding finishing touches to it. Just as framing highlights the finished portrait, refinements highlight the portfolio of work. At this stage, both the teacher and student take a final look.

During this stage, students examine the entire portfolio for visual inconsistencies (missing labels, torn or tattered artifacts) or for refinements that might improve the outward appearance or the inherent meaning of particular artifacts. This is the time to spruce up the cover, check the registry for accuracy, and add artwork or design ideas that give the final flair that makes the difference between a solid effort and an exemplary one.

Teachers may want to use this stage to evaluate the portfolio, develop and apply scoring rubrics, and assign a grade or grades to the portfolio. Although not every teacher will want to grade or be required to grade portfolios, it is helpful to understand the grading process.

Introduction

"Portfolios offer a way of assessing student learning that is quite different from traditional methods. While achievement tests offer outcomes in units that can be counted and accounted, portfolio assessment offers the opportunity to observe students in a broader context: taking risks, developing creative solutions, and learning to make judgments about their own performances" (Paulson, Paulson, & Meyer, 1991, p. 63).

The issue "to grade—or not to grade" portfolios is probably the most controversial and confusing of all the decisions related to portfolio use.

The issue "to grade—or not to grade" portfolios is probably the most controversial and confusing of all the decisions related to portfolio use. The key to understanding the options available is to review the purposes of the portfolio. If the purpose of the portfolio is to reflect on the students' best work, to establish a process and product for conferences, or to trace growth and development in an informal way, the portfolio does not have to be evaluated.

If, however, the portfolio is tied to accountability and is, therefore, an evaluation tool, individual pieces or the portfolio as a whole need to be assessed according to predetermined performance standards. Kallick (1989) says learners have to "internalize external standards and expectations for good work and understand explicit ways to improve performance to meet those standards" (p. 313).

If the portfolio is used schoolwide, Wiggins (cited in Vavrus, 1990) suggests that colleagues should decide on the key items that represent important learning and set some standards for what constitutes excellent work along with indicators that cover the range of students' needs, interests, or styles.

The following methods are just some of the many options for evaluating portfolios.

Ideas

No Grades
Personal Satisfaction—"I'm Growing!"
Some portfolios are used to show students' growth and development over time, their reflections about their work, and their rationale for selecting specific pieces. Since this work reflects the students' choices, the portfolio is not graded. The teacher, parents, and peers, however, can provide oral and written comments to the students.

Many teachers, especially at the elementary level, feel that grades cause students to focus more on "What did I get?" rather than "What did I learn?" They also feel that students' comfort level, willingness to take risks, and self-esteem increase when they are *not* worried about receiving an evaluation on their work. Some educators feel that eliminating grades from items in the portfolio also encourages more honesty in peer comments and more constructive feedback from parents and teachers. In this type of portfolio, individual effort and development are emphasized instead of comparisons with other students. Students with linguistic, learning, or behavioral challenges and students who prefer different learning styles usually feel good about their portfolio because it represents their personal favorites, demonstrates what they have learned in a variety of formats, and allows them to have fewer time constraints than with traditional tests and assignments. This type of portfolio provides a way to organize student learning into a manageable and attractive unit that

Many teachers, especially at the elementary level, feel that grades cause students to focus more on "What did I get?" rather than "What did I learn?"

provides a richer experience than hundreds of loose worksheets, drawings, or tests.

Graded

Previously Graded Entries—"What Did I Get?"

Many portfolios contain a selection of items that may have been previously graded. The items have been turned in earlier in the quarter and assessed according to grading standards established by the district, teacher, and/or students. Sometimes the grading is done with rubrics—guidelines for giving scores based upon performance criteria and a rating scale. For example, if students receive a grade for cooperation within their groups, the rubric could look like the following:

CRITERIA: COLLABORATION IN COOPERATIVE GROUP

Elements	Indicators			Score
Interaction	• Little interaction	• Some interaction	• Enthusiastic interaction	2
	1—————————2—————————3			
Conversation	• Not always focused on topic	• Usually focused on topic	• Involved conversation on topic	3
	1—————————2—————————3			
Involvement	• One student involved	• Several students involved	• Entire group involved	2
	1—————————2—————————3			
On-Task Behavior	• Several students off task	• One student off task	• All students on task	3
	1—————————2—————————3			

Scale:
10–12 = A
6–9 = B
4–5 = C

Final Score: **10**
Final Grade: **A**

Figure 21

Since all the work in this type of portfolio has already been graded, the portfolio is used to review student work, to trace growth and development, and to conduct conferences. Sometimes students revise and refine their previously graded work to increase the quality of their entries before sharing the portfolio with others. They can staple both copies together to show the corrections they have made.

Key Items Selected for Grading—"Roulette Wheel"
Sometimes teachers tell the students in advance which entries will be graded once the portfolio is submitted. Teachers might select two items which they feel are important (e.g., research paper, cooperative project, oral presentation) and then allow students to select two or three other items to be graded. This method allows teachers to make sure key pieces are included, while also allowing students to choose which pieces they feel will earn the highest score. It is important that the items be graded according to predetermined criteria and indicators developed by the teacher and students. Some teachers, however, choose another option. They do *not* tell the students which items they plan to grade until after the entire portfolio is submitted. These teachers want students to do quality work on *all* of the entries—not just the ones they know will be graded. Once the key items are selected, they are usually assessed using a rubric.

> Sometimes students revise and refine their previously graded work to **increase the quality of their entries before sharing the portfolio with others.**

Criteria: Visual Aid for Presentation

Elements	Indicators			Score
Size	• Too small to be seen by anyone	• Could be seen by some	• Large enough to be seen by all	2
	1————————2————————3			
Color	• No color	• Some color	• Very colorful	3
	1————————2————————3			
Design	• No graphics	• Some graphics	• Creative graphics	2
	1————————2————————3			
Content	• Did not pertain to speech	• Pertained to speech	• Reinforced main ideas of speech	2
	1————————2————————3			

Scale:
10–12 = A
6–9 = B
4–5 = C

Final Score: **9**
Final Grade: **B**

Figure 22

Each Entry Graded—"One to One"

Every item in the portfolio may be graded either *prior* to submitting the final portfolio or *after* the portfolio is submitted.

Every item in the portfolio may be graded either *prior* to submitting the final portfolio or *after* the portfolio is submitted. The grades are determined by standards developed by the class and teacher or from scoring rubrics established by the school or district. The evaluation scale helps ensure consistency and fairness in the grading process. The *advantage* of this method is that students put a great deal of effort into all the entries since they know they will be evaluated. This type of portfolio often constitutes a large percentage of the total grade. Students usually know in advance what assignments will be graded and the criteria upon which they will be evaluated. The *disadvantage* for teachers is the time involved in assessing all the portfolios when they are submitted, especially in the middle school and high school where teachers may teach more than 150 students. The following example shows an evaluation of a videotaped speech that was included in the portfolio. (See Figure 23.)

© Harris Reprinted with permission.

SPEECH SCORING RUBRIC—INDIVIDUAL ENTRIES
(videotape in portfolio)

Name of Speaker _____

Title of Speech _____

VOLUME

				SCORE
I couldn't hear you.	It was hard to hear you.	I heard you most of the time.	You were easy to hear.	
1	2	3	4	

EYE CONTACT

				SCORE
You didn't use eye contact.	You hardly ever used eye contact.	Sometimes you made eye contact.	You had really good eye contact.	
1	2	3	4	

VISUAL

				SCORE
Foul Ball (You had no visual or it wasn't right.)	A Walk (Your visual was good, but you didn't use it.)	R.B.I. (Your visual made your speech better.)	Grand Slam (Your visual was very creative.)	
1	2	3	4	

FOCUS

				SCORE
Muddy (I wasn't sure what you meant.)	Foggy (Sometimes I didn't know what you meant.)	Fuzzy (Most of the time I knew what you meant.)	Crystal Clear (I always knew what you meant.)	
1	2	3	4	

Comments: _____

_____

_____

_____

Scale
14–16 = A
10–12 = B
7–9 = C
Below 6 = Not yet

Final Grade: _____

Figure 23

IRI SkyLight

Many teachers are finding that regardless of whether or not individual items in the portfolio are graded, they can grade the whole portfolio on the basis of specific criteria.

One Grade for Whole Portfolio—"Blue Ribbon"

Many teachers are finding that regardless of whether or not individual items in the portfolio are graded, they can grade the whole portfolio on the basis of specific criteria such as creativity, completeness, organization, evidence of thoughtfulness, evidence of improvement, reflectiveness, and quality of work. Teachers can then assign a letter grade, point value, or percentage grade based upon the organization of the entire portfolio. This type of grading does not require as much time as grading each item, but it still produces quality work. Often a rubric is used to specify criteria and guidelines.

SAMPLE CRITERIA FOR GRADING PORTFOLIOS

Accuracy of Information
Completeness
Connections to Other Subjects
Creativity
Development of Process
Diversity of Selections
Evidence of Understanding
Following Directions
Form (Mechanics)
Growth and Development
Insightfulness

Knowledge of Content
Multiple Intelligences
Originality
Persistence
Quality Product
Reflectiveness
Self-Assessment
Timeliness
Transfer of Ideas
Variety of Entries
Visual Appeal

Others:

Figure 24

Weighted Portfolio Rubric—"And Justice for All"

Often the items in a portfolio are not equal in importance and, therefore, should not be weighted the same when determining the final grade. Assessments of the entire portfolio can be constructed to value the criteria that are most important. A portfolio can also be weighted according to what the teacher and students feel are the most important criteria.

High Stakes Accountability Portfolio—"High Stakes"

Many states are experimenting with portfolio assessment at the state level. These so-called "high stakes portfolios" assess state goals achieved by the students. Outside scorers assess the portfolios using scoring rubrics that have been developed by psychometricians and teachers to increase the reliability of the scoring process. The portfolio includes required entries that demonstrate that the student has met certain requirements.

Combination Portfolio—"Potpourri"

Teachers can combine all these grading options or alternate them for different times of the year and for different purposes and types of portfolios. Many standardized rubrics from school systems, districts, and states are available to use as models and preparation guidelines so teachers can align classroom expectations and assessments with standardized and global expectations and assessments.

Final Thoughts about Grading Portfolios

Regardless of whether or not portfolios are graded or whether teachers or outside evaluators assess the contents, portfolios present a portrait of a student that cannot be captured by checklists, anecdotal records, or report cards. According to Vavrus (1990), "The key to scoring a portfolio is in setting standards relative to your goals for student learning ahead of time. Portfolios can be evaluated in terms of standards of excellence or on growth demonstrated within an individual portfolio, rather than on comparisons made among different students' work" (p. 48).

"Portfolios can be evaluated in terms of standards of excellence or on growth demonstrated within an individual portfolio, rather than on comparisons made among different students' work."

Examples: Perfect and Evaluate—Sample Portfolio Rubrics

Final Portfolio Rubric
(No Grades)

Student: _Jim B._   Grade: _3rd_   Date: _June 1_

Selection	Teacher Comments
1. Problem-solving log	You used several methods to solve the problems.
2. Book report video interview	Your answers to the questions I asked were excellent.
3. Artwork	Try to use more color in your work.
4. Peer-edited short story	The comments others made really helped your story.
5. Cassette of the reading	Your fluency and enthusiasm have improved.
6. Science experiment drawing	The explanation of your drawing was right on target.

Final Portfolio Rubric
(Each Item Graded)

Student: _Carol B._   Class: _Geometry_   Date: _May 26_

Selections	Grade	Comments
1. Geometric drawings	95	You have done a beautiful job drawing and labeling the angles.
2. Research report on "Why Math"	89	The research you did on the relevancy of math helped you see its importance.
3. Reflective journals	90	Your frustration on tests is evident from your journal. You seem to be working through your anxiety.
4. Profile of math-related professions	90	You made the transfer of math from the classroom to the outside world.
5. Student self-evaluation for course	91	I gave myself an 91 because I like math, but I still can't solve problems on my own.
Total Points 455 ÷ 5 = 91	91	It's interesting that your average is the same as your own self-evaluation!

Comments: Your writing and research skills and appreciation of why math is important are excellent. Even though you feel math is your weakest subject, you are making great strides to overcome your phobia and solve problems.

Suggested Future Goals: Work with your group more. Ask them to "talk out loud" when they are solving problems so you can see their thought processes.

Average grade for class work = 83 (33%)
Average grade for quizzes and tests = 85 (33%)
Final portfolio grade = 91 (34%)
Final grade for class = 86—B

(Adapted from Burke, 1993)

One Grade for Entire Portfolio Rubric

Directions: Fill in the indicator under each score.

Criteria	Does Not Meet Expectations 1	Meets Expectations 2	Exceeds Expectations 3	Total Score
Organization				
1. Creative Cover	✓			1
2. Self-Assessment			✓	3
3. Completion of All Items			✓	3
Visual Appeal				
1. Layout		✓		2
2. Art/Graphics			✓	3
3. Creativity		✓		2
Evidence of Understanding				
1. Knowledge of Subject		✓		2
2. Reflections			✓	3
3. Application of Ideas			✓	3
Form				
1. Sentence Structure		✓		2
2. Grammar		✓		2
3. Spelling/Punctuation			✓	3

Scale: 30 - 36 = A   Total: 29 / 36
25 - 35 = B
12 - 21 = C
0 - 12 = Not Yet

Final Grade: B

Weighted Portfolio Rubric

Student: _James_   First Quarter

1	2	3
Little Evidence	Some Evidence of Originality, Creativity, and Content	Strong Evidence

1. Creative cover and table of contents   1 ② 3   x 5 = 10 (15)

2. A cooperative research project   1 2 ③   x 8 = 24 (24)

3. A video of a performance   1 2 ③   x 7 = 21 (21)

4. A log, journal, or metacognitive activity   1 ② 3   x 5 = 10 (15)

5. An original graphic organizer   1 2 ③   x 4 = 12 (12)

6. A self-assessment of portfolio and statement of future goals   1 2 ③   x 4 = 12 (12)

Total 89 (99)

Scale: 69 - Not Yet
70 - 74 = D
75 - 83 = B
84 - 89 = B
90 - 99 = A

Final Grade: B

Comments: _You did an excellent job on your group project and video performance. You need to work on creating an original cover that reflects your creativity. Your logs and journals are not as reflective as they could be._

IRI SkyLight

TEACHER PLANNER

Create a Rubric

Directions: Select a project, performance, or portfolio and list three criteria for assessing the assignment, three key *elements* that make up the criteria, the *scoring scale*, and the *indicators* that describe what a student has to do to earn each score.

Student: _____ Course: _____ Grade: _____
Assignment to be assessed: _____

1. **CRITERION:** _____   **SCORE**

     Scale   1——————————— 2 ——————— 3

Elements	**Indicators**			
a. ☐	• _____	• _____	• _____	____
b. ☐	• _____	• _____	• _____	____
c. ☐	• _____	• _____	• _____	____

2. **CRITERION:** _____

            1——————————— 2 ——————— 3

a. ☐	• _____	• _____	• _____	____
b. ☐	• _____	• _____	• _____	____
c. ☐	• _____	• _____	• _____	____

3. **CRITERION:** _____

            1——————————— 2 ——————— 3

a. ☐	• _____	• _____	• _____	____
b. ☐	• _____	• _____	• _____	____
c. ☐	• _____	• _____	• _____	____

Total Score: ☐

Comments: _____

Scale ☐   (27)

_____

_____   Final Grade: ☐

IRI SkyLight

©1994 by IRI/Skylight Publishing, Inc.

Blackline

PORTFOLIO RUBRIC

Name: _____ Subject: _____ Grade: ____

Directions: Develop criteria and indicators for assessing the final portfolio.

Criteria	Does Not Meet Expectations 1	Meets Expectations 2	Exceeds Expectations 3	Total Score
[ ]				
1.				
2.				
3.				
[ ]				
1.				
2.				
3.				
[ ]				
1.				
2.				
3.				
[ ]				
1.				
2.				
3.				

Comments:

Scale:

Total Score:
_____
36

Final Grade:

IRI SkyLight

©1994 by IRI/Skylight Publishing, Inc.

Blackline

CHAPTER 8:

CONNECT AND CONFERENCE

"The trouble with most of us is that we'd rather be ruined by praise than saved by criticism."
—Norman Vincent Peale
(cited in Peter, 1977, p. 417)

CONNECT AND CONFERENCE

Overview

A portfolio by its very definition is a case to hold things in. And although not explicitly stated in the definition, it is implied that the case is used to carry the items about for others to see.

Just as artists' works are viewed and appreciated by others, students' portfolios must also go on display for others to see. In an artist's life, experts in the field and other interested parties, such as patrons of the arts or aficionados of a particular period or style, take this opportunity to not only view the work, but to scrutinize the work and offer informed critiques of their assessments. Students, too, have the opportunity for input from others as they present their works in a three-way portfolio conference with the teacher and their parents. All the intricacies of the portfolio work come to surface, as the dialogue unfolds among the interested parties.

Introduction

"Evaluation continues the spirit of inquiry by providing one more chance to ask questions—and one more opportunity to learn. Evaluation occurs as learners take reflective stances in relation to their work and then invite others in to have conversations about it." (Crafton, cited in Crafton & Burke, 1994, p. 5)

Through ongoing critiques and conversations about the portfolio collection, students develop the capacity to become truly reflective learners.

"AFTER 20 YEARS OF SCHOOLING, YOUR APTITUDE TEST SHOWS THAT YOU'RE SKILLED AT JUST ONE THING--TAKING TESTS."

© Schwadron Reprinted with permission.

It is at this stage of "connect" when all the students' activities in acquiring knowledge and capacities for self-reflection on learning processes culminate in the true essence of portfolios—"to value." Through ongoing critiques and conversations about the portfolio collection, students develop the capacity to become truly reflective learners "who always act with intention" (Harste, Woodward, &

Burke, 1984). This stage helps the students move beyond test-taking skills to gaining reflective skills.

If teachers' purposes have been to assist students in becoming more thoughtful in setting goals and evaluating the outcomes of learning and social processes, as well as reflective in expressing ideas, this stage of communicating the contents of portfolios to various audiences will be essential. As reflective inquiry occurs through conversations with teachers, peers, and others, students learn to see their learning experiences in different ways. "The talk, the listening to the perspectives, gives us new choices and a fresh opportunity to position ourselves differently in the world" (Crafton, 1994, p. 6).

Portfolio conferences range from simple, one-on-one dialogues between students and teachers, or students and parents, to formal exhibitions that promote student conversations about the contents of the portfolio with varied audiences. Whether conferences are basic or complex, they need to be well-planned, monitored, and evaluated for their capacity to meet their established purposes.

To effectively plan portfolio conferences, teachers need to consider the purposes for portfolio conferences. Next, they make decisions about who the audience will be and when the conferences will take place. Once this is determined, they are ready to engage students in planning the remainder of the process. In this chapter, the types of conferences will be examined in order to select those that best meet the purposes.

At this point the *what* and *how* of the conference are mapped out:
- What will the goals be?
- What reflections do learners need to engage in?
- What questions should they prepare for their audience?
- How do they wish to evaluate the conferences?

Finally, the conference will be planned. Dates need to be scheduled and setup needs (if any) arranged. Strategies for introducing the portfolio or inviting questions from the audiences are prepared ahead of time. Students should practice trying to anticipate the types of questions that will be asked and formulating appropriate responses.

The same ongoing teacher guidance that earlier supported the self-reflection process is needed to prepare students for confer-

Portfolio conferences range from simple, one-on-one dialogues between students and teachers, or students and parents, to formal exhibitions that promote student conversations about the contents of the portfolio with varied audiences.

ences. Students need to consider how to present each artifact or the overall content of their portfolios to their audiences. Through the conversations at the portfolio conference, the student often demonstrates that he or she has become a reflective and autonomous learner "who self-initiates, problem solves, reflectively evaluates her learning, collaborates, and shows concern for others, and engages in complex thinking strategies" (Crafton, 1991, p. 94).

Ideas

Why Have Portfolio Conferences?

Portfolio conferences allow people other than the student and the teacher to see and discuss a student's work. They also provide real evidence of the accomplishment of schoolwide or districtwide objectives. Portfolio conferences also promote student goal setting and communication among teachers and parents. Most importantly, they engage students in meaningful reflection, inquiry, and discussion about their own learning processes.

The following ideas can help guide teachers in considering the purpose, audiences, number, nature, and outcomes of portfolio conferences.

Conferences Promote Ongoing Student Evaluation and Goal Setting—"On and On"

Teachers plan for ongoing conferences with students (or between students) when they wish to promote student evaluation and inquiry into student learning processes. Teachers can also use these ongoing conferences to promote student monitoring of their progress toward personal goals. "Despite all the testing that we do, both formal and informal, only the learner really knows what has been learned" (Howell & Woodley, cited in Goodman, Bird, & Goodman, 1992, p. 87).

Conferences Promote Student-Teacher Communication—"Can We Talk?"

When teachers value students' dialogue about learning and achievement, they will schedule regular conferences where students select final artifacts, complete learning logs or biographies of works, or make additions to their learning lists. These conferences help students to reflect on their accomplishments, "recognizing how successful they were, and facilitating new experiences where they can apply their learning" (Silvers, 1994, p. 27).

When teachers value students' dialogue about learning and achievement, they will schedule regular conferences where students select final artifacts, complete learning logs or biographies of works, or make additions to their learning lists.

Conferences Promote Student-Student Communication—"Two-Way Talk"

When portfolios are collected by cooperative groups, entire classes or entire schools, teachers will initiate student dialogue. This dialogue might focus on the quality of the learning-community experience and the artifacts that reflect the goals and purposes of these portfolios. Conferences will be group-based and engage the social and cognitive skills that are promoted in the cooperative learning classroom.

Conferences Promote Student-Parent-Teacher Communication—"Threesomes"

The portfolio allows the student to be part of the parent-teacher conference. When the student enters the dialogue, the parent-teacher conference becomes more learner-centered. The student plans, conducts, and evaluates the presentation of artifacts to parents, and the teacher monitors the conference, facilitates the dialogue at key places, and encourages the student to be responsible for its success.

Conferences Promote Teacher Accountability—"High Standards"

In schools where teachers must provide evidence of student achievement, portfolio conferences can be scheduled for students, teachers, and other school faculty. These conferences demonstrate the quality of the student's products, the depth of his or her reflections, and the significance of his or her learning. These portfolio conferences connect the parallel processes of restructuring schools toward higher standards with the accomplishment of authentic learning and assessments.

Conferences Promote Parental Satisfaction—"Parent Talk"

As many schools move toward learner-centered curricula and instructional practices, one of the greatest challenges is informing parents of these practices and explaining the professional and scientific knowledge base that supports the adaptation of these practices. Portfolio conferences can address the concerns of parents by demonstrating their child's overall learning and achievement.

Portfolio conferences enable parents to see and hear about their child's real learning, which includes engaging in hands-on activities, solving increasingly difficult problems, and working cooperatively with others. Parents who observe the active learning process and

Portfolio conferences can address the concerns of parents by demonstrating their child's overall learning and achievement.

interview students who display artifacts of their learning become less cautious, more trusting, and often more enthusiastic about the evolving school curriculum.

Conferences Accompany Community-Wide Exhibitions—"Links"
The portfolio conference is instrumental in promoting important connections between students and parents, family and community members, and concerned local business people. Although community-wide exhibitions often remain an unrealized vision, they offer the potential to reestablish the critical links between schools and families and between schools and communities.

As school faculties and their students become more confident with portfolio assessments and conferences, schoolwide exhibitions may become as commonplace as the science fair is today. Technology makes it possible to create computer-stored portfolios of student written work and multimedia presentations. Already, some school districts can provide selected exhibitions of students' computer-stored portfolios through modem to gathered community or business groups.

Technology also makes it possible for teachers to use software that transforms student written or graphic work and photographs of products or projects into computer-stored portfolio data files. Laser-disc video will make it possible for students to conduct portfolio conferences with community members or "pen pals" from across the world. Hand-held scanners make it possible for teachers to collect and download information on student learning as they are engaged in it. Teachers can collect and store checklists, anecdotal, observations, and self-evaluations in a few minutes. These breakthroughs lend an air of expectancy to the possibility of better engaging students, teachers, parents, and community members in a dialogue throughout the learning process and especially at the time of portfolio conferences.

What Is the Focus of the Conference?
Significant Achievement—"It Counts!"
These conferences give students the opportunity to present portfolios of their significant achievements across selected areas of the curriculum. These might include pieces that promote student reflection on teacher-graded work, selected learning logs, projects or performances, or significant improvements in standardized test scores.

> **Although community-wide exhibitions often remain an unrealized vision, they offer the potential to reestablish the critical links between schools and families and between schools and communities.**

Goal Setting—"Goal Post"

These conferences focus on students' previously set goals and include self-assessments of how they have reached their goals. Portfolios include pieces that highlight how the student has matched, met, or surpassed his or her goals. In some instances, the student may select a "not yet" piece and discuss the strategies he or she will employ to achieve the goal in the future.

Responses to Single Learning Process Areas—"Invitational"

In these conferences, students compile portfolio artifacts that reflect each indicator of a particular process (such as becoming an effective writer). Students use the criteria that were originally applied to scoring and reflect on how they have developed in these areas. They might include several artifacts to represent different audiences and invite response through conference guides created ahead of time.

Personally Satisfying Pieces—"I Like It!"

Students select pieces that are most satisfying to them as learners and use this conference to display how they have grown as readers, writers, group members, intelligent thinkers, or overall great students. While the portfolio pieces they share in the conferences might represent many or only a few of the subject areas or learning processes, the pieces should represent achievements that the student feels best about.

Joint Work with Others—"Join In"

These portfolio conferences often are used to communicate the group, class, or schoolwide purposes. Here students present how they have succeeded as communities of learners in a variety of cooperative projects and learning experiences.

Overall Portfolio—"The Big Picture"

This is perhaps the most important conference, because it requires the student to reflect on and self-assess strengths, weaknesses, successes, and failures. This conference represents the "holistic picture" of his or her performance and disposition toward learning.

In this conference, the student calls attention to those pieces that best represent him or her throughout all the selected areas. The student may write a summary for each selection, or create a conference guide that explains his or her characteristics as a learner. "The Big Picture" encourages students to value themselves for all the things they are.

> **Students select pieces that are most satisfying to them as learners and use this conference to display how they have grown as readers, writers, group members, intelligent thinkers, or overall great students.**

After determining the purpose of the portfolio conference and type of conference, the teacher and the student should decide *who* will participate in the conference and *when*.

Who Is Involved and When Do They Conference?

After determining the purpose of the portfolio conference and type of conference, the teacher and the student should decide *who* will participate in the conference and *when*. Fortunately, portfolio conferences blend quite seamlessly with traditional parent conference meetings or end-of-the-marking period pauses in curriculum and instruction. Depending on the purpose, teachers may select the *who* and *when* of portfolio conferences from a full palette of choices.

Connections to Authentic Learner Involvement—"Connecting"

Student-Student	Monthly
Pen-Pal ("Tech-Pal")	Quarterly
Multi-Age Student	By Semester
Student-Parent-Teacher	Quarterly
Portfolio Exhibition—Everyone	Year-End

Teacher Accountability—"Accounting"

Student-Teacher	Monthly
Student-Parent-Teacher	Quarterly
Student-Parent	By Semester
Portfolio Exhibition—Everyone	Year-End

Parental Satisfaction with Learner Performance—"Pleasing"

Student-Teacher	Monthly
Student-Student	Quarterly
Student-Parent Home Conferences	By Semester
Student-Parent-Teacher	Quarterly
Portfolio Exhibition—Everyone	Year-End

Outside Evaluations of the Success of Teaching and Learning—"Evaluating"

Student-Student (Cooperative Group Members)	Monthly
Multi-Age Student	Bimonthly
Student-Parent Home Conferences	By Semester
Significant Other	Quarterly
Pen Pal ("Tech Pal")	Quarterly
Schoolwide/Community-Wide Portfolio Exhibitions—Everyone	Year-End

How Does the Conference Happen?
Planning for the Portfolio Conference

To effectively prepare for the portfolio conference, students and teachers must begin with a plan. They must set goals, think about invitations, plan schedules, and set up strategies as well as plan how to evaluate the conference.

Conference Goals—"Goalie"

At this point it becomes important to decide what the goals for the conferences will be. What do learners (and teachers) need to know? What stories do they want to tell? What do they want their audience to know about them as learners? What outcomes would they like to result from their conferences?

Learner Reflections—"Reflective Fair"

Students and teachers also need to decide the nature of reflections they will use throughout the conference. What reflections do learners need to engage in? Should they prepare reflective questions or stem statements for their audience?

Invitations—"Invites"

Students need to think about how they will invite their "guests" to portfolio conferences. Carefully selected invitations should tell guests the purposes and themes of the conference. Should students design brief, informal invitations? Should they write a formal letter which includes information of what to expect and even some suggestions for conference protocol? Teachers can promote learner responsibility and autonomy by allowing students to consider these questions and formulate and implement a plan.

Planning the Set-Up—"Book It"

Finally, the conference details need to be planned. Dates should be scheduled, and setup needs (if any) arranged. Strategies for introducing the portfolio or inviting questions from the audience should be prepared ahead of time. Students may also rehearse their list of questions, stem statements, or prompts to anticipate the nature of their responses.

Scheduling—"On Time"

The students can be engaged in making decisions about these questions and even be given some of the responsibilities for the preparations (setting up the schedule and writing the invitations). In the case of student-student conferences, cooperative groups can

Should they write a formal letter which includes information of what to expect and even some suggestions for conference protocol?

work to create schedules for in-school presentations. When parents or others are invited for specific time-period conferences, students may contact parents to find out when they are available. In planning for whole class or entire school exhibitions, students can work within time allotments provided by teachers to plan the length of presentations.

Set Up—"Blueprints"

Teachers can also engage students in planning the room arrangement or set up of the rooms needed for portfolio conferences. Students may create "blueprints" for display tables that will showcase artifacts from portfolios, or other products and projects. They may also want to create signs to direct guests from the entry doors to the conferences or exhibitions.

Conference at Home —"Scheduling Problems"

Sometimes parents cannot attend portfolio conferences in person because of scheduling conflicts. Many teachers send home the portfolios along with a Guideline Sheet that describes how the parents can conduct the conference at home. Sometimes teachers include sample questions to help parents start the process as well as a form for parents to respond to their feelings about the portfolio and the conference.

During the Portfolio Conference

During the conference, students must incorporate their "show and tell" skills. This includes introductions, questioning strategies, and thoughtful responses.

Introducing, Initiating, and Responding—"Intros"

If students are planning conferences for the first time, they may need some guidance in considering how they will introduce their portfolios, how they will initiate the communication with their audiences, and how they might respond to comments or questions that they may not have anticipated. By promoting student thinking about these social skills, teachers can ensure that each student will have the opportunity to practice or role play some typical or atypical scenarios which may occur in parent-student or significant other-student conferences.

Protocol—"Conference Etiquette"

This may also lead students to establish some conference guidelines or protocol for the benefit of their audiences. Once again, the more autonomy students are given to prepare their portfolios and conference formats (within the established purposes) the more likely they will be to accept and maintain ownership of their learning processes.

Using Questions at Conferences —"The Million Dollar Question"

Different questions target different conference goals.

SAMPLE QUESTIONS TO ASK AT PORTFOLIO CONFERENCES

Goal-Setting Conference
Type: Single Learning Process
(Reading)

1. How do you want to grow as a reader?

2. What strategies will you work to improve?

3. What are your goals for the next quarter?

Student-Teacher Conference
Type: Personally-Satisfying
Pieces

1. Select one of the items in your portfolio and tell me why you selected it.
2. Do you notice a pattern in the types of pieces you like the best? Explain.
3. If you would have included your "least satisfying" pieces, what would they be and why?

Student-Parent-Teacher Conference
Type: Significant Achievement

1. Explain why you included some of these items.
2. In what area have you achieved the greatest improvement? Why do you think you have improved so much?
3. Which one of your achievements surprises you the most? Why?

Student-Student Conference

Type: Joint Work with Others

1. How do you feel about working in groups?
2. What was the biggest challenge of group work?
3. On which project or performance did your group do the best? Why?
4. If you could redo any group project, what would it be and why?

Figure 25

The more autonomy students are given to prepare their portfolios and conference formats (within the established purposes) the more likely they will be to accept and maintain ownership of their learning processes.

Conference Dialogue—"The Rehearsal"
Using the two sample dialogues (Figures 26 and 27) as models, students rehearse their conferences.

> "We use port-
> folios at this
> school be-
> cause there
> are so many
> things that we
> are interested
> in learning
> that they all
> just can't be
> shown by the
> tests we
> take."

STUDENT-LED PARENT-TEACHER CONFERENCE
Significant Achievement

Student: Let me begin my portfolio conference by telling you a little bit about our portfolios and what the purpose has been since we began using them. Then I want you to look over some parts of it and ask me anything you would like.

Parent: All right. That sounds great.

Student: We use portfolios at this school because there are so many things that we are interested in learning that they all just can't be shown by the tests we take.

Parent: Excuse me, you mean you don't use your tests for grades any more.

Student: (laughing) No, I wish! I have some tests in my portfolio—that you'll see—but getting back to the purpose—we agreed that our portfolios would show us and you that we are learning important things in science, math, social studies, and other things. But also that we're learning how to solve problems, to write about things that are important to us, and to become better at working on big projects or ideas together. So our portfolios are about our achievement in all our subjects—but also about who we are as people. For this conference, we all decided that we would choose pieces from our whole portfolio that show "significant achievement."

Parent: These are things you got your best grades on?

Student: Not always, but most of the time. Let me show you this math paper (takes a paper from folder). I selected this one and wrote my reasons here. Do you want to read it?

Parent: Yes. (Reads. Then looks at attached math sheet.) So, you really figured out how to do this kind of problem, even though you got many problems wrong on the quiz.

Student: Yeah. It was when we were going over our mistakes in peer study groups that I figured it out! It was a great feeling!

Parent: I'm jealous. I wish that would have happened to me in algebra.

Student: What can I tell you—I just got what it takes—ha, ha! Anyway, all the rest of the things in my portfolio are like this. They show I've learned, but they also show how and sometimes why. Let's look at some other pieces and you can ask me whatever you want to know.

The teacher participated as an observer. He stopped by and greeted the conference attendees. He listened briefly, but urged them to continue unless they had a question.

Figure 26

TEACHER-STUDENT PORTFOLIO CONFERENCE
Personally Satisfying

Teacher: I see you're ready to begin your portfolio conference. I'm impressed already. Your cover is great!

Student: Thanks! I got a little carried away—but I like the way it looks. It's really wild.

Teacher: Tell me about it and then let's talk about what's inside.

Student: Well, since this was our personally satisfying portfolio conference, I got to wondering. If I got an award for each best work that was one of my favorite things, what would each award be?

Teacher: Hmm. I like that idea!

Student: So, I pasted on the ticket stubs from the baseball game my dad took us to—and then a card of my favorite player. Here's a picture of my favorite dessert—yes, chocolate! Here's a picture from my favorite vacation—and everything else.

Teacher: This is fun to look at. Let's see what you've put inside.

Student: (Somewhat apologetic.) Well, it was hard to choose work from my working portfolio that was my best, because my opinion changes.

Teacher: I'm glad you noted that. I like that you did include this writing assignment from September. It was very good.

Student: Thanks, I know it was the best. It makes me feel good to look at it now because I remember working hard on it with the computer. It's easier for me to write when I type it instead of writing. It looks better when it's done.

Teacher: Don't give up on your handwriting. It gets better all the time. Can you also show me a piece that you think shows work on learning an idea or about an important issue or event that was satisfying to you?

Student: (Pausing to think.) Umm. Oh yes. I'll show you the science presentation that I did with my group. You remember. . .

Figure 27

"It makes me feel good to look at it now because I remember working hard on it with the computer."

Students may likely choose to prepare surveys or informal stem statements to request feedback from those who have conferenced with them.

Post-Conference Evaluation

Following the portfolio conference, an evaluation is needed as the final step. Both the teacher and the student may participate. An example of a post-conference evaluation is on page 113.

Evaluations—"So What"

It is also important for students to think ahead to the "so what" of the conferences. How will they know if they were successful in meeting their goals? How do they wish to evaluate the conferences? What would they like to learn by the end of the conference? Students may likely choose to prepare surveys or informal stem statements to request feedback from those who have conferenced with them.

Examples: Connect and Conference

PREPARING

Portfolio Conference Goals Set by Students

Primary
I want my portfolio to tell my story about how I learned to read this year.

Intermediate
By the time my parents are done looking at my portfolio and talking to me about my work and the reflections I have written, I want them to be as excited as I am about how much I have improved in everything!

High School
My portfolio conference should show the teachers in this school that I have really learned how to use computers to organize and present a project on communications.

DURING

Introductions: Welcome to Our Portfolio Conference

Dear Honored Guest:

Welcome to our fifth grade portfolio exhibition. We are pleased that you have joined us as we present the portfolios of the significant work we have achieved during the past year.

We have worked hard to select just the right pieces for our portfolios. We think they tell you the "real story" about who we are as students here at Whitman School.

Here are some suggestions we thought you would like to use as you visit each of our exhibits. Feel free to use any of them and to spend as much time as you like at our exhibits.

Have a good time and thank you very much for coming tonight.

Sincerely yours,

Whitman School Fifth Grade Class

DURING

Introductory Initiating Responses— Portfolio Conference Protocol for Audiences

The following are some tips that the students from our school have designed to help you get the most from your portfolio conference. We hope you enjoy visiting with our students. Please remember to complete the survey about your impressions before you leave. Thank you.

- Listen to the student.

- If responses are unclear, please ask for more information.

- Concentrate on one piece at a time.

- Make comments about the portfolios that can help students to look at their work from new perspectives or to value their work from another person's view.

- Ask students to tell you how they feel about their work at Washington Elementary.

POST

Evaluation of Portfolio Conference

Student Name: ____*Brian*____   Grade Level: __*8*__

Conference Date: __*11-14*__

1. What were your goals?
   To share my portfolio with my parents.

2. List the goals you achieved.
   Covered all items. Answered their questions.

3. How do you feel about the conference(s)?
   Great! It's over!

4. Think of one suggestion you received during a conference that you know you want to try.
   More artwork.

5. Rate your overall portfolio conference(s).

|————————————|————————————|————⊙—|
Not Yet   Pretty Good   Yes! Yes! Yes!

TEACHER PLANNER
FOR PORTFOLIO CONFERENCES

1. **Who will participate?**

   _____

   _____

   _____

2. **What type of portfolio conference will be planned?**

   _____

   _____

   _____

3. **What are the goals of the conference?**

   _____

   _____

   _____

4. **Logistics:**

   A.   Date: _____ Time: _____ Place: _____

   B.   Invitations: _____

   _____

   C.   Room setup: _____

   _____

   D.   Refreshments: _____

   _____

5. **How will you evaluate the conferences?**

   _____

   _____

   _____

IRI SkyLight

©1994 by IRI/Skylight Publishing, Inc.

PORTFOLIO CONFERENCE QUESTIONS

Directions to students: Using the Three-Story Intellect Verbs as a guide, construct seven questions that you would like to be asked by the teacher, fellow students, or your parent(s) or guardian(s) during your portfolio conference. Try to include questions from all three stories and questions about academic achievement, processes, cooperative projects, and outside interests.

1. _____

_____

2. _____

_____

3. _____

_____

4. _____

_____

5. _____

_____

6. _____

_____

7. _____

_____

**THREE-STORY INTELLECT VERBS:
A GUIDE FOR
CONSTRUCTING PORTFOLIO
CONFERENCE QUESTIONS**

3 APPLYING
Evaluate
Imagine
Judge
Predict
Speculate
Apply A Principle   If/Then
Some other words for application are...   Estimate   Forecast

2 PROCESSING
Compare   Reason
Sort   Contrast
    Solve
Distinguish
Explain (Why)
Classify
Some other words for processing are...   Analyze
Infer

1 GATHERING
Count
Describe
Match
Name
Recite
Select
Some other words for gathering are...   Recall
Tell

IRI SkyLight

Blackline

PARENT PORTFOLIO CONFERENCE GUIDE

Dear Parent: Please review your son's/daughter's portfolio and ask them questions about their work. The following questions might help start the discussion. Thank you for your cooperation.

1. What have you learned about yourself by putting together your portfolio?

2. What is your favorite piece? Why?

3. If you could publish one thing in this portfolio, what would it be and why?

4. Select several items and tell how you feel about them.

Please write any comments you have and give to your son/daughter to return to school.

_____

_____

_____

_____

_____

Signed: _____ Date: _____

CHAPTER 9:

INJECT/EJECT TO UPDATE

"The great artist is the simplifier."
—Henri Frédéric Amiel (cited in Peter, 1977, p. 27)

INJECT/EJECT TO UPDATE

Overview

Although the focus of the portfolio is often the parent conference, ideally the portfolio process extends beyond that immediate goal to a long-range goal (Wolf, 1989). In its ultimate form, the portfolio becomes a true collection of work over time that the students continue throughout their school career and beyond. Students who use a portfolio as part of their college entrance and career interview processes continually inject artifacts into and eject artifacts out of their portfolio so the portfolio is always up to date and reflects their past and current work.

This continual process of injecting new items and ejecting outdated work fits nicely with the term, "processfolio." "Processfolio" implies that work is constantly in progress, ever-changing and developing, shifting direction and focus as the various academic and career paths are targeted. Sometimes it is necessary to rework the portfolio to meet a new or different purpose. And it makes sense to include the most current work as part of an entire collection of personal artifacts.

This continual process of injecting new items and ejecting out-dated work fits nicely with the term, "processfolio."

Just as artists find it beneficial to continually rearrange and even redesign their portfolios to keep them current, fresh, and inviting, students also may want to reap the benefits of periodic updates and renovations to their portfolios. Although most people know why it is valuable to keep a résumé current, most people do not understand why it is important to keep the portfolio current. However, more and more colleges, universities, and employers survey portfolios during the entrance or performance review process.

Introduction

"Whatever the medium, the message is the same: thinkers and inventors often keep longitudinal collections of their ideas, drafts and questions. They use them as a kind of storehouse of possibilities, valuing them as a record of where they have been and reading them for a sharp sense of their own signatures and uncertainties" (Wolf, 1989, p. 37).

A portfolio can be likened to a revolving door (Fogarty, 1994). The concept of the revolving door conjures up the images of constant motion as the doors circle around, ejecting passengers on one side

118

and injecting others on the opposite side. The dynamics are unending, with continuous change to the norm. The dynamics of portfolio development are not as hurried and flurried as people moving in and out of a revolving door, but the concept of change inherent in the revolving door is definitely a crucial part of the portfolio process.

The portfolio registry is key to handling this mode of injecting current material and ejecting outdated material. The registry is used to log in items and log out others, just as guests sign the hotel registry.

Considerations that influence how the portfolio registry is used include a number of typical models: the periodic cleanup done weekly, monthly, or quarterly; the momentary make over that spruces up the portfolio for an unexpected view; the not-so-routine facelift that targets areas for radical changes and new dimensions; or the serendipitous refresher that evolves as a special piece is added that sparks a creative change.

The portfolio registry is key to handling this mode of injecting current material and ejecting outdated material.

Ideas

Types
Periodic/Routine Checking—"Dental Checkup"
This is the most common mode for the injection and ejection of material. The checkup can be a regularly scheduled activity, just like a periodic dental checkup. The checkup helps clean things up and helps to monitor overall status. This is often orchestrated by the teacher, who has set predetermined benchmarks and guidelines for portfolio management.

Depending on the age of the students and the purpose and type of portfolio, the checkup may happen weekly, monthly, quarterly, or biannually. During these routine reviews, students perform a mini-selection process accompanied by a reflection on the various items and a look at the connections to both long- and short-term goals. In fact, during the routine checkups, the entire portfolio procedure is replicated in a short, condensed version. However, the main purpose of the checkup is to inject current items and to eject others.

Update—"Momentary Make Over"

Sometimes unexpected occurrences call for a makeover of the portfolio or its contents. For example, special guests may be scheduled to visit the classroom or student teachers may be stopping in to check the writing folders. It's just like life outside of school—when someone calls to say he or she will be stopping by, everyone scurries to tidy up the house. So the unexpected event in the classroom may also sound the alarm for a speedy run through the portfolio.

Change Direction—"Major Face-lift"

Sometimes the inject/eject cycle is triggered by the need for a new "look." For example, as students ready themselves for a round of college entrance visits, an all-important job interview, or a final review of the year, a complete cosmetic change as well as an interior renovation may be needed.

For someone who is making a career shift or is entering a new or alternate field of work, a major portfolio face-lift may be needed. Although this may not seem pertinent to the younger student, the portfolio should be seen as an integral tool for lifelong learning. The key to performing a face-lift is to focus on the purpose and goals of the portfolio. What do I want to happen as a result of this portfolio review? Let the answer act as the guide to your changes. This may include redesigns of the container, cover, organizational plan, page layout, registry, and anecdotes. Each change should naturally emphasize the new direction of the portfolio.

Implement—"Spring Cleaning"

When new work is injected into the portfolio, older work may no longer fit. Thus, the inject/eject cycle begins again. For example, as a student adds her puppet to the portfolio, she may suddenly think about the early sketches and the script that was used with the puppet play. She realizes that this might be a great artifact to use as a "biography of a work" (Wolf, 1989). So, she gathers items that depict the evolution of the puppet, and in so doing, refreshes this section of the portfolio. By adding the "biography" pieces, she may need to eliminate some other pieces just to keep the number of items manageable.

For someone who is making a career shift or is entering a new or alternate field of work, a major portfolio facelift may be needed.

Examples: Inject/Eject

ROUTINE CHECKUP

Item in? <u>Social Studies Relief Map</u>
Item in? <u>Audiotape of Rap for</u>
          <u>Unit on DNA</u>

— — — — — — — — — — — —

Item out? _____
Item out? _____

Comment: I'm not really ready to take anything out, but I did consider it.

MAKE OVER

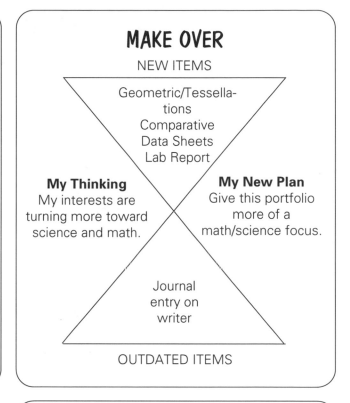

NEW ITEMS

Geometric/Tessella-
tions
Comparative
Data Sheets
Lab Report

My Thinking
My interests are
turning more toward
science and math.

My New Plan
Give this portfolio
more of a
math/science focus.

Journal
entry on
writer

OUTDATED ITEMS

FACE-LIFT

OLD
I have geared my
portfolio toward
editing skills and
my writing talents.

**NEW
DIRECTION
(Design and
Computer)**

**OLD
DIRECTION
(Editing and
Writing)**

NEW
I want to emphasize
my design skill and my
knowledge and expertise
on the computer.

SPRING CLEANING

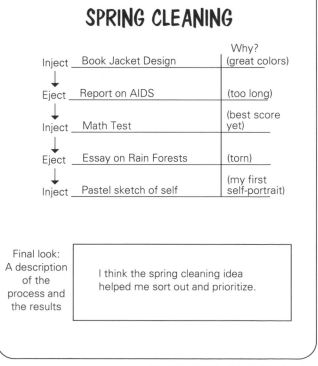

		Why?
Inject	Book Jacket Design	(great colors)
Eject	Report on AIDS	(too long)
Inject	Math Test	(best score yet)
Eject	Essay on Rain Forests	(torn)
Inject	Pastel sketch of self	(my first self-portrait)

Final look:
A description
of the
process and
the results

I think the spring cleaning idea
helped me sort out and prioritize.

©1994 by IRI/Skylight Publishing, Inc.

TEACHER PLANNER

Review your portfolio system and comment on when and for what reasons you could use the Inject/Eject system.

Dental Checkup: (To do routinely scheduled cleanups)

Momentary Make Over: (To update)

Major Face-lift: (To change direction or focus)

Spring Cleaning: (To improve or refine)

SPRING CLEANING

Directions for students: Periodically browse through the portfolio. Add items when appropriate. But don't forget to take some out.

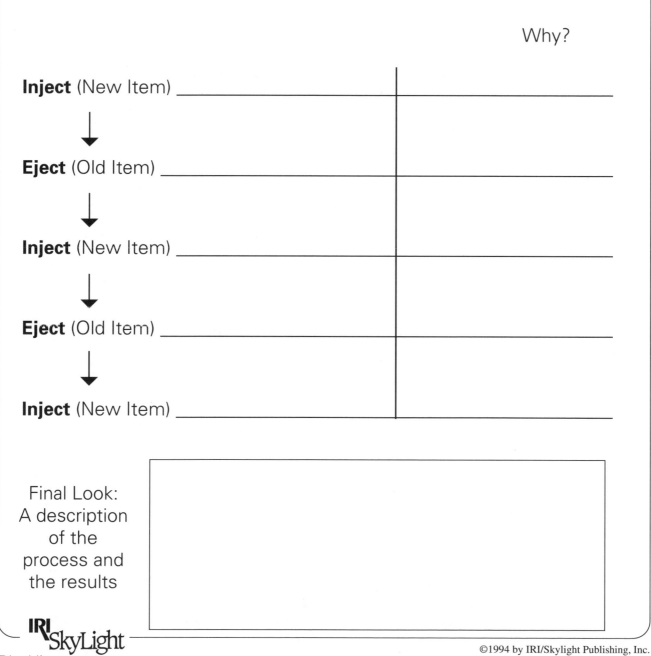

Why?

Inject (New Item) _____

↓

Eject (Old Item) _____

↓

Inject (New Item) _____

↓

Eject (Old Item) _____

↓

Inject (New Item) _____

Final Look:
A description
of the
process and
the results

IRI SkyLight

Blackline

NOTES:

_____

_____

_____

_____

_____

_____

_____

_____

_____

_____

_____

_____

_____

_____

_____

_____

_____

_____

_____

_____

_____

_____

_____

CHAPTER 10:

RESPECT ACCOMPLISHMENTS

"Everything is art if it is chosen by the artist to be art."
— **Samuel Adams Green (cited in Peter, 1977, p. 27)**

RESPECT ACCOMPLISHMENTS

Overview

It is understood that the primary purpose of portfolios in the schools today is to enhance the assessment process. By including actual artifacts that evidence students' development, assessment extends beyond test scores or arbitrary grade point averages. The values and myriad uses for portfolios are beginning to surface as they are used in more and more schools. Students may also find that portfolio exhibitions are a viable tool to use in other circumstances.

Just as the artist yearns for a gallery showing of her accumulated pieces, students at every level of schooling yearn to show off their portfolio and its artifacts. The portfolio exhibition is an artistic event that calls for the students to skillfully present their work and communicate their talents to others. The exhibition brings the work alive. As students present their pieces to others, viewers gain valuable insight into the persons behind the work.

This chapter is devoted to the art and skill of exhibiting a portfolio. Exhibitions extend beyond the parent conference, but the ideas suggested here can also be used during that initial conference.

Introduction

"Product exhibitions . . . allow students to demonstrate their ability to apply knowledge and skills in authentic contexts" (Ferrara & McTighe, 1992, p. 341).

The exhibition is the time when "the rubber hits the road" and the critics come to the showing. The portfolio presentation is also the time for the creator to make her work come alive. Among the considerations necessary to prepare for the presentation are: the primary goal, the target audience, the allotted time frame, media options, personal style, and other pertinent concerns (e.g., openers and closers).

The teacher and students need to determine the primary goal(s) of the conference. Is the presentation for college entrance? a job interview? a peer conference? Is it a critique by one's mentor? Regardless of the established purpose, it is prudent for presenters to review all they know about the anticipated audience. What are they looking

The portfolio exhibition is an artistic event that calls for the students to skillfully present their work and communicate their talents to others.

for? How are they going to view the work? Are they familiar with the type of work? Is there a particular format to follow? Are they expecting a portfolio presentation? What can be done to maximize their interest and understanding?

The time frame should also be determined. Will there be time for the "full metal jacket" or just a "Ready? FIRE. Aim," shotgun approach. What media will be used? Is there a video segment or an audiotape that needs to be included? If media is part of the presentation, how is it to be incorporated in the overall plan?

Another factor that needs to be considered is the personal style of the presenter. What are the other possible ways for sharing with others? Students may need to select an appropriate presentation, rehearse as needed in front of a mirror, and practice before a trusted friend or relative.

"I hope this isn't another ploy to raise your grade, Haskell."

© Bouthillier Reprinted with permission.

To plan the most effective presentation, the goal must be clearly defined.

Ideas

Elements

Goal Setting—"Scoring the Goal"

Getting the portfolio ready is only one part of the story. To plan the most effective presentation, the goal must be clearly defined. Is the primary goal one of self-evaluation and self-reflection through the sharing with peers or parents? Or is the primary goal a summative evaluation by the teacher? Or is the goal to inform and impress a third party about the talent of the person presenting the portfolio?

Whatever the goal may be, students need to zero in on it. The student may use this formula to set his or her goal:

1. Write the goal in a journal or notebook to clarify it in your mind.
2. Dialogue with a partner to articulate the goal in your own words.
3. Discuss the goal with a teacher or a parent.
4. Visualize the presentation and see yourself achieving the goal.

Audience—"Audience Audit"

Dale Carnegie's famous book, *How to Win Friends and Influence People* (1981), advocates the idea that to reach a goal, a person must first understand others' goals or find out what the other party wants and be sure to deliver it. Students must know who their audience will be and plan to meet the expectations of this audience. Whether it's a parent conference, a teacher evaluation, or a job interview, they need to think about what the audience will be looking for and how they can best highlight those things.

> **Students must know who their audience will be and plan to meet the expectations of this audience.**

AUDIENCE AUDIT

Possible Audiences	Probable Focus
Parent(s)	Areas of progress and growth
Teacher	Evidence of required work, quantity and quality
Guidance Counselor	Areas of strengths and weaknesses
Personnel Director	Skills, quality, creativity, versatility
Peers	Quality, quantity, special artifacts that reveal personality and interests
Admissions Officer	Academic pride, talents, and skills

Figure 28

Time—"Hang the Time Frame"

Nothing is worse than a presentation that drones on for too long. To avoid making a boring presentation, students need to "refocus." The portfolio speaks for itself in many ways, but the speaker needs to bring the overall portfolio alive. Care must be taken to target, rehearse, and actually present within a predetermined time frame.

"Hang the Time Frame," is a simple strategy to keep students on track. Students hang up a sign that gives the allotted time. Somewhat like a cue card, the sign reminds the student presenter to be succinct and brief. Once the time frame is hung, a peer can audit the time for a partner as they practice the presentation. Practicing with this time frame technique provides a great opportunity to hone skills and develop emphasis where desired.

Audio/Visual—"Media Event"

As the presentation is being prepared, the media question is sure to pop up. Will there be any media in the presentation? film? video? slides? audiotape? multimedia? computer software? If the answer to any of these options is yes, the presenter must attend to media logistics. Students should carefully plan the elements for a media presentation, or disaster may follow.

Students may employ de Bono's (1992) PMI strategy to decide if using media is a good idea. By appraising the pluses (P), minuses (M), and interesting (I) aspects of media presentation, students can have a better idea of what they may need to plan for in their media presentation.

Personal style includes how the students present themselves in both public and private situations.

PORTFOLIO MEDIA PRESENTATION

PLUS	
MINUS	
INTERESTING	

(de Bono, 1992)

Figure 29

Personality—"What's Your Style?"

Personal style includes how the students present themselves in both public and private situations. Some may prefer a lighthearted approach, using humor to diffuse the tension that is part of any formal gathering. Others may feel more comfortable presenting in a genuine, folksy way, sprinkling the presentation with personal anecdotes. Still others may choose a reserved style, relying on the strength of the portfolio to carry the show. And, some may select a direct approach to the presentation, dotting the monologue with pointed questions.

Students should ask themselves questions about their style. What's my style? Is it humorous, lighthearted, folksy, reserved, or direct? One way to find out is to videotape a rehearsal of the portfolio presentation for the student to analyze and reflect upon. Another way is to have students work with partners and assess each other's style through peer dialogue.

Openings and Closings—"Gotcha"
In the final analysis, the presenter makes or breaks his or her presentation in the first ninety seconds. With that in mind, the student needs to understand the importance of the first artifacts to be reviewed and the opening monologue. Students should select the material with care.

In the final analysis, the presenter makes or breaks his or her presentation in the first ninety seconds.

ELEMENTS TO CONSIDER FOR OPENERS:

Surprise
Elaboration
Exquisite Quality
Originality
Mystery
Quote(s)

Figure 30

A strong close is also effective in making a memorable presentation. The closing might include many of the same elements that work as openers. Also, students can use surprise, elaboration, quality, originality, mystery, quotes, sketches, cartoons, or graphics to cinch the close.

TO CINCH THE CLOSE . . .

Mystery
Quotes
Sketches
Cartoons
Graphics
Questions

Figure 31

Examples: Respect Accomplishments

SCORE THE GOAL

GOAL:

STEPS:

AUDIENCE AUDIT

☐ Parent(s)

☐ Teacher

☐ Guidance Counselor

☐ Peers

☐ Personnel Director

☐ Admissions Officer

☐ Other

HANG TIME FRAME

MEDIA EVENT?

☐ Audiotape

☐ Videotape

☐ Multimedia

☐ Slides

☐ Computer Display

☐ Other _____

☐ Other _____

Media in Portfolio Presentation

P	
M	
I	

IRI SkyLight

TEACHER PLANNER
CHECKLIST FOR EXHIBITIONS

☐ **Date** _____

_____

☐ **Time** _____

_____

☐ **Place** _____

_____

☐ **Invitations** _____

_____

☐ **Refreshments** _____

_____

☐ **Equipment** _____

_____

IRISkyLight

Blackline

EXHIBIT YOUR WORK

Student Name: _____

Directions to Student: Think about each element and jot down your thoughts.

Scoring the Goal:

Audience Audit:

Hang the Time Frame:

Media Event:

What's Your Style?

Openings/Closings:

WHAT'S YOUR STYLE?

Graph Your Ideas Yourself

	Humorous	Lighthearted	Folksy	Reserved	Direct	Other _____	Other _____
10							
9							
8							
7							
6							
5							
4							
3							
2							
1							

IRI SkyLight

Blackline

CONCLUSION

The development of a portfolio system, as presented in this book, is a complex process that requires commitment to long-term change. Some may use the system as outlined from beginning to end; others may "dip in" and pull out selected sections to meet specific and urgent needs for their personally relevant projects-in-progress; still others may resequence the steps, omit steps, or even add steps of their own.

Regardless of how you use this book, it is our hope that you understand the portfolio system. To help you visualize the portfolio system, this conclusion provides an example of one type of a completed portfolio. This integrated portfolio on a thematic unit illustrates what an actual student portfolio might look like.

By browsing through the collected and selected items and by noting the thoughtful reflections on each artifact, the ideas discussed in this book become more concrete. Notice how the sample portfolio parallels the elements of the portfolio system advocated in the ten-step process in this book. This is an *academic* portfolio with a focus on grading a specific unit of work.

Sample Portfolio
Project purposes and types
The purpose of the integrated thematic portfolio is to evaluate a student's academic skills in a unit on Greek mythology and to share ideas with others during conferences and an exhibition.

Collect and organize
Students collected all their work throughout the unit on Greek mythology and stored it in their working portfolios (hanging file, cereal box, notebook). They kept pictures and descriptions of projects, cassette recordings and videos of performances, and copies of all their work in language arts, mathematics, social studies, science, art, and physical education.

> **The development of a portfolio system is a complex process that requires commitment to long-term change.**

135

Select key artifacts

At the end of seven weeks of the Mythology Unit, students selected artifacts from their working portfolio according to the categories decided upon by the teachers involved. The categories included the following: one poem, one original science myth, one group project, a mathematics entry, an art project, a social studies entry, a biography of a work, a self-assessment, and a free pick. The students then decided which entry to submit under each category.

Interject personality and signature pieces

The original cover of the portfolio and the artwork, the design, and the layout of the portfolio demonstrate the personality of each student. The use of color, graphics, tone, and mood distinguishes one portfolio from another and one individual student from another.

Reflect on each piece metacognitively

Note the reflections and labels on the various entries in the portfolio. Students reflected on their feelings about the piece, the reactions they received from peers, and sometimes what they would do differently if they redid the piece.

Inspect to self-assess and align to personal goals

Note the specific sheet used to list short- and long-term goals of students in light of their inspection of the portfolio (p. 151). This entry allowed students to evaluate their progress in reaching personal or academic goals and adjust or redirect their course of action as their needs changed.

Perfect and evaluate and grade (if you must)

Specific pieces in the portfolio have already been graded throughout the quarter. The teachers and the students, however, decided they wanted another grade for the whole portfolio based upon the criteria they thought were important. The classes created their own rubric for self-assessment, peer-assessment, and teacher assessment to evaluate the following criteria: creative cover, completeness, form, creativity, evidence of understanding, and reflection. (See page 149.) After completing the rubric, students also completed stem statements to provide a narrative self-assessment entry. (See page 150.)

Connect with others and conference

Students were asked to generate a list of questions they would like to be asked about their portfolios (p. 153). These questions were given to peers, teachers, parents, and guests at the conferences and

> The original cover of the portfolio and the artwork, the design, and the layout of the portfolio demonstrate the personality of each student.

exhibition to stimulate ideas and discussion. The students practiced asnwering questions by role-playing parents, teachers, or personnel directors prior to the actual conference.

Inject/eject to update
The artifact registry (p. 152) allowed students to review their work on a regular basis and make additions and deletions as needed to keep the portfolio fresh and up-to-date. The artifact registry is most useful in a year-long portfolio in order to keep the contents manageable and to allow students to "change direction" as their needs and goals change throughout the year.

Respect accomplishments and show with pride
Even though conferences allow students to share their portfolios with a few other people, sometimes it is exciting to share work with a much broader audience. A classwide or schoolwide exhibition showcases all the students' portfolios, projects, and performances. Other students, parents, school staff, and members of the community are invited to visit the exhibition, talk with participants, share ideas, and celebrate learning. (See page 154.)

Portfolio as a Palette

> "Art begins with resistance—at the point where resistance is overcome. No human masterpiece has ever been created without great labor."
>
> Andre Gide (1869-1951)
> "Poetique"
> Bartletts

The portrait presented by the portfolio, the conferences, and the exhibitions is a richer, more vibrant representation of the whole student than the picture provided by report cards and standardized tests alone.

Portfolios can help paint a picture of a student as a lifelong learner. The portrait presented by the portfolio, the conferences, and the exhibition is a richer, more vibrant representation of the whole student than the picture provided by report cards and standardized tests alone. Despite the "great labor" involved in developing and maintaining a portfolio system, the "human masterpiece" that evolves from the process—a student involved in his or her own learning—is truly a work of art.

STUDENT PORTFOLIO PROFILE

Student: _Mindy M._ **Grade:** _8th_ _First Quarter_

Purpose: _To show growth and development over a quarter, to give a grade for_

the whole portfolio, and to share during conferences and an exhibition.

Type of Portfolio: _Integrated Thematic Portfolio on Greek Mythology_

Subject Areas: _language arts, mathematics, social studies, science, art, and physical education_

Process:	Time Frame (12 weeks)
1. Collection of work for working portfolio	_7 weeks_
2. Selection of pieces for final portfolio	_2 weeks_
3. Reflection and self-assessment	_1 week_
4. Conferences and exhibition	_2 weeks_

Selection Process: Teacher selects *categories* of entries: one poem, one original science myth, one group project, an integrated assignment, a mathematics entry, an art project, one social studies assignment, a biography of a work, and a self-assessment. Students may select which entry to submit for each category.

Method of Evaluation: one grade for whole portfolio (rubric)

Criteria for Evaluation: creative cover, completeness, form, creativity, evidence of understanding, reflection

MY PORTFOLIO
GREEK MYTHOLOGY UNIT

**"Beware all mortals who
gaze at me alone!
Use a mirror to reflect,
or you will turn to stone!"**

Mindy "Medusa" Smith—Grade 8

GREEK MYTHOLOGY UNIT

My Portfolio
Table of Contents

"THE FIRST SUPER BOWL ON MT. OLYMPUS"

There once was a football coach named Zeus
Whose sportsmanship and morals were loose
He would lie and he'd cheat
Every team he would meet
Until Athena would call a truce.

The Greek Gods of Old Olympic High
Were conceited and quick with a lie
They'd toy with mortal men
In vain attempts to win
And on gold winged sandals they would fly.

Poseidon charged with trident in hand
Chased by the Olympus Marching Band
The next one to follow
Was Captain Apollo
Selling his newest sun lotion brand.

The mortal Greeks in the scrimmage fell
And were cast by Hades into hell
They soon began to plot
And place kicked a lot
And formed their own league—The NFL.

The Greeks took the field for the final game
To crush the Gods was the mortals' aim
The Gods endured the boo's
The Greeks wore Nike shoes
The first Super Bowl brought the Greeks fame!

—Mindy Medusa

Reflection:
*I really enjoy writing poetry
—especially funny poems. I
try to use rhyming words
that are interesting. It's hard
with limericks because you
have to have three words
that rhyme. I'd like to write
jingles for ads on television
someday. I don't know
what other jobs require
poetry writing.*

1

BIOGRAPHY OF A WORK
ITEM: LIMERICK—THE FIRST SUPER BOWL ON MT. OLYMPUS

Date	Summary
9/17	Teacher assigned a poem about Greek mythology. We could choose any type of poetry we wanted.
9/19	I started writing about the first pep rally at Olympus High using aabb rhyme scheme. Frustrating!
9/21	Didn't like the poem—It was too "sing-songy." Decided to change to limerick with aabba rhyme scheme.
9/23	Wrote *five* drafts of poems. Used ˘ / ˘ / ˘ / ˘ / symbols to count syllables in each line to make sure I had 9-9-6-6-9 in each line. Very time consuming!
9/25	Typed poem on computer and cut out pictures to put on it. Wish I could draw better.
9/27	Read poem to the class and they thought it was Awesome! The class wants to make it into a skit to show at the exhibition.

Reflection
I think this poem is one of my best pieces. It's funny, creative, and it shows how much I know about the gods and goddesses. It also shows that I know how to write limericks—and they are not easy!

2

PHYSICAL EDUCATION

GROUP PROJECT OF OLYMPIC GAMES

Our group selected events used in the Greek Olympics and demonstrated what the events looked like. We selected the 10 meter race and discus throw and took a video of what the events looked like (video in portfolio).

Of course, I had to pretend I was a boy because girls did not participate in the early Olympics and they were not allowed to attend.

Reflection: This is not our best work. The filming of the video was difficult because we didn't use a tripod. The camera moves around too much and is sometimes out of focus. We need to learn how to edit a video. Also, our script wasn't very good. Our narrator ran out of things to say!

3

THE MODERN-DAY LABORS OF HERCULES

Hercules was a Greek hero who was hated by Hera. Hera made Hercules go crazy and in a fit of rage he killed his wife and children. The famous 12 labors he was forced to perform were a penalty for his crimes. If Hercules were alive today, the following "Herculean tasks" could be assigned to him by Hera:

Labor 1:   Make Hermes, the god of magic, reduce the U.S. deficit.

Labor 2:   Bring back Elvis from the rock-and-roll underworld.

Labor 3:   Reduce the Hydra-headed evils of drugs and violence in our cities.

Labor 4:   Clean out the Augean sewers of New York.

Labor 5:   Wrestle the god San Andreas and tie him down to prevent more earthquakes along the fault line in California.

Labor 6:   Capture the winds of Aeolus in a bag to prevent hurricanes from hitting Florida.

Labor 7:   Bring back the head of Madonna, the goddess whose looks turn men to stone.

Labor 8:   Wrestle the evil Hulk Hogan in the land of Wrestlemania.

Labor 9:   Capture the evil Harpie Sisters and cancel their syndicated talk show.

Labor 10: Fight the three-headed monster Barney who guards the entrance to "Toys R Us."

Labor 11: Harness the fire-breathing reindeer of "Santataur" from the land of the North Pole and make them bring the chariot of gifts to our school.

Labor 12: Level the plains of Woodstock and sow salt so that no music festival can "spring from the earth" again.

> **Reflection:** I'm not too happy with this piece. At first I was going to be serious and have the modern-day Hercules conquer real problems. Then I tried to be humorous. I think I ended up somewhere in between. Should have added more artwork to this piece.

4

ORIGINAL MYTH TO EXPLAIN
"How We Got Lightning Bugs"

There once was a snotty Greek youth named Bugga. He was always playing practical tricks on people. He would sneak around during the night at drive-ins and flatten chariot wheels of couples who were kissing. He used to sneak up on the mortals and the gods in the dark and pull his childish pranks.

One day, however, Bugga played a trick on the wrong god. Bugga was sitting behind the stables of Mt. Olympus one night watching the nymphs prepare Apollo's horses to drive the sun chariot to bring up the sun for the new day. While no one was looking, he placed tiny walkman transistors in the horses' ears. Apollo soon arrived at the stables in all his golden splendor. The sun god radiated fire and power as he boarded his chariot, hooked up the sun to the back end, and prepared to take his daily ride to bring up the sun for the world.

When he left the stable, the horses charged ahead wildly out of control. Apollo used all his godly powers to restrain them. For you see, Bugga had inserted *heavy metal* tapes into their walkmen and the horses, crazy from the sound, were plunging toward earth and a fiery collision.

Apollo was finally able to control the fierce beasts and bring them and the sun back safely to Mt. Olympus. When he returned, he heard snickering coming from the bushes, and he uncovered Bugga laughing hysterically. Apollo realized the prank Bugga had played, and he knew he would have to punish the young punk for almost burning up the earth.

"Bugga, you think you're pretty cool, don't you?" whispered Apollo.

"What, old dude, I don't know what you're talking about," Bugga whined.

"You won't be sneaking around in the dark anymore to play your tricks. Everyone will know when you are around."

With that comment, Apollo struck Bugga with his lyre and Bugga shrunk to a small flying bug. Apollo touched the bug again, and this time Bugga's tail lit up.

"Now," laughed Apollo, "try to sneak around at night. Your glow will give you away. People will capture you in their hands and imprison you in jars. You'll be a firefly! And since you like that horrible heavy metal music so much, I'll curse you so you can never hear again!"

And to this day whenever you see a firefly—it's really Bugga. But don't try to yell to him. He can't hear you!

Reflection: I need to work on my dialogue. It doesn't sound natural yet. I also want to edit this story. I tend to be too wordy. I think I can have the same effect by "tightening up" the story. I also need to work on the ending.

5

MATH

MATH PROBLEM USING PYTHAGOREAN THEOREM

Pythagoras was a Greek mathematician who was born around 500 B.C. He later founded a school to promote the study of natural science, philosophy, and mathematics. He is most famous for discovering the relationship beween the lengths of the sides of a right triangle. I can use this theorem to find unknown lengths of a triangle.

> Pythagorean Theorem—In any right triangle with legs a and b, and hypotenuse c, $a^2 + b^2 = c^2$.

Problem: Find c, the length of the hypotenuse.

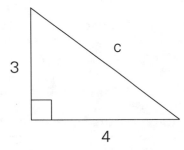

Solution:

$$a^2 + b^2 = c^2 \qquad \text{Write the theorem.}$$
$$3^2 + 4^2 = c^2 \qquad \text{Substitute values for variables.}$$
$$9 + 16 = c^2$$
$$25 = c^2$$
$$\sqrt{25} = c$$
$$5 = c$$

The hypotenuse, c, has a length of 5.

Check:
$$a^2 + b^2 = c^2 \qquad \text{substitute values}$$
$$3^2 + 4^2 = 5^2$$
$$9 + 16 = 25$$
$$25 = 25$$

> Reflection: I'm still not too sure where I will ever use this in life. I will have to think of a word problem to write. I just know I can now verify right triangles and find missing values of right triangles.

6

ART

PRODUCTS FROM MYTHOLOGY

Ajax—Mighty Greek Warrior
and Sink Cleanser

Midas —A King with the
Golden Touch and a
Muffler

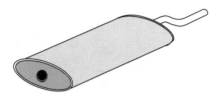

Trident—Poseidon's
Symbol and Gum

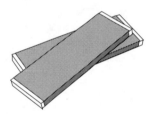

Mt. Olympus—Palace of
Gods and Olympic-sized
swimming pools

Titans—Original
Gods and Large
Ship (Titanic)

Mars—Roman God of War
and Candy Bar

Helios—Sun God and
Helium Balloons

Reflection: I can't draw! Thank goodness for cut-out art and computer graphics. I'd love to take an art class as an elective. It would be fun to sketch and draw.

7

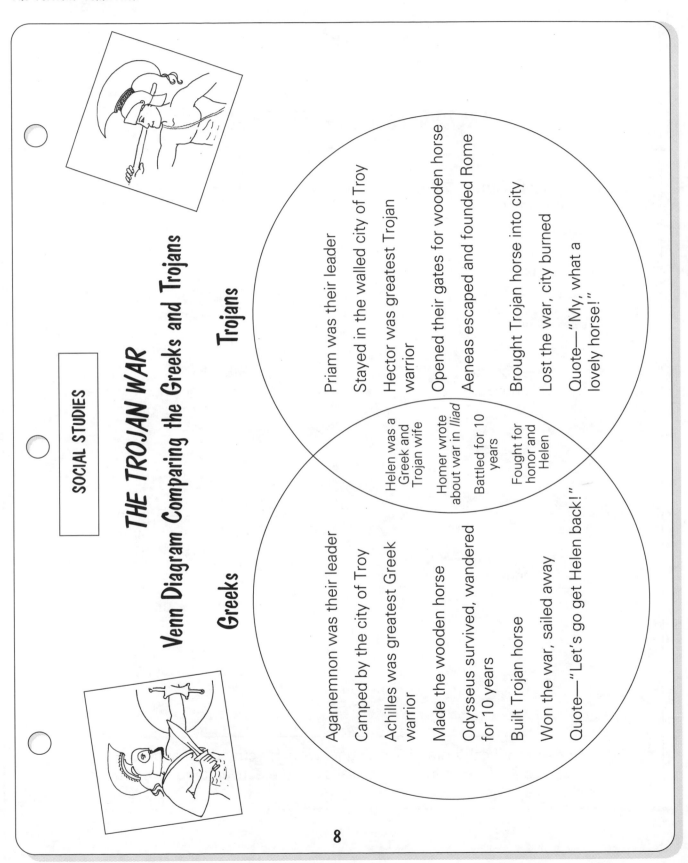

SOCIAL STUDIES

THE TROJAN WAR
Venn Diagram Comparing the Greeks and Trojans

Greeks

Trojans

Agamemnon was their leader

Camped by the city of Troy

Achilles was greatest Greek warrior

Made the wooden horse

Odysseus survived, wandered for 10 years

Built Trojan horse

Won the war, sailed away

Quote—"Let's go get Helen back!"

Helen was a Greek and Trojan wife

Homer wrote about war in *Iliad*

Battled for 10 years

Fought for honor and Helen

Priam was their leader

Stayed in the walled city of Troy

Hector was greatest Trojan warrior

Opened their gates for wooden horse

Aeneas escaped and founded Rome

Brought Trojan horse into city

Lost the war, city burned

Quote—"My, what a lovely horse!"

8

PORTFOLIO RUBRIC

☑ Self   ☐ Peer   ☐ Teacher

		Hades	**Parthenon**	**Mt. Olympus**
		1	2	③
1.	Creative cover	The Underworld Gazette	The Athens Chronicle	The Olympus Sun
		1	2	③
2.	Completeness	Minotaur (half man, half bull)	Perseus (half man, half god)	Zeus (all god)
		1	②	3
3.	Form (spelling, grammar, punctuation, sentence structure)	Dionysus (Sloppy—god of wine)	Odysseus (Needs help—phone home)	Hermes (Great—god of alphabet)
		1	②	3
4.	Creativity	Touched by mere mortals	Touched by the demigods	Touched by the god of creativity
		1	2	③
5.	Evidence of understanding	Hercules (Where are my Cliff Notes)	Apollo (I see the light)	Athena (Goddess of wisdom)
		1	2	③
6.	Reflection	Medusa (Never uses a mirror)	Narcissus (Gazes at own image only)	Aphrodite (Reflects in mirror on regular basis)

Comments: I know I still need to work on my sentence structure—but sometimes it gets in the way of creativity. I really don't get grammar rules. "They're Greek to me!"

Total Points: 16 = A

Scale: Total 18 pts.
15 – 18 = A
10 – 14 = B
 6 – 9 = C
Not Yet

9

149

SELF-ASSESSMENT OF PORTFOLIO

STEM QUESTIONS

1. What is your favorite piece? Why?

My favorite piece is my limerick about the first Super Bowl on Mt. Olympus. I've always liked to write funny poems, but no one ever saw them. Now the whole class likes my poems. They've asked me to write a poem about our football team to read at the next Pep Rally. I'm really excited.

2. What piece is least satisfying to you? Why?

The group project where we videotaped some of the events from the Olympic Games. We weren't very organized and our camera work wasn't good. Sometimes it's harder to get things done right when five people have to agree. We need more team-building skills!

3. If you could share this portfolio with anyone living or dead, who would it be?

I would like to share my portfolio with my grandmother because she used to read me stories from a mythology book when I was young. I didn't like fairy tales as much as the stories of the gods and goddesses. I grew up loving Greek mythology and I'd like to share this portfolio with the person who inspired me.

10

GOAL-SETTING:
MY SHORT-TERM GOALS

Goals	Target Date
1. I need to learn how to use spell check and grammar check on my computer.	Jan. 20
2. I need to find out how to write better reflections. Mine all say about the same thing.	March 6
3. I need to find out *when* I would use the Pythagorean theorem—I don't understand why it's important.	By next test

MY LONG-TERM GOALS

Goals	Target Date
1. I want to learn how to do more computer graphics to help the layout of my portfolio and my other work.	Jan. 27
2. I want to work on my group skills. I lost my patience with group members when we did our video.	Feb. 3
3. I would like to take some elective courses in creative writing.	1996

Date of next conference: _April 3_   Signed: _Medusa Mindy_

11

ARTIFACT REGISTRY

Student_____*Mindy*_____ **Grade**_____*8th*_____ **Date**_____*10/5*_____

DELETIONS

Date	Item	Reasons
10/5	Math problem using Pythagorean Theorem	I didn't understand when and why I would need to use this.
10/5	Group project of Olympic Games Video	Poor quality. Picture moved around. Bad sound. Lots of pauses.

ADDITIONS

Date	Item	Reasons
10/5	Word problem using Pythagorean Theorem	I wrote a problem about buying fencing for my yard. Made more sense.
10/15	Group video of interviews of athletes after races	We learned how to use camera better and we wrote a good script for interviewer and athletes.

12

QUESTIONS FOR PORTFOLIO CONFERENCE

Student:_____Mindy_____   Date: _____Oct. 5_____

I have prepared the following questions that peers, parents, or teachers could ask me about my portfolio during the conference.

1. If you could become one of the mortals or gods from Greek mythology, who would you become and why?

2. If you could select one item from this portfolio to share with the whole student body, what would it be and why?

3. What subject area do you think you need to work on most? Why?

4. What do you think was the major contribution the Greeks gave the world? Explain your answer.

5. If you could board a time machine and go back to 5th century Greece for a day to interview anyone, who would it be and why?

6. Compare the fall of Troy to the fall of the Roman Empire, fall of Germany, or fall of Saigon.

7. Explain this quotation: "Beware of Greeks bearing gifts."

8. If you lived in 5th century Greece, would you rather live in Athens or Sparta? Explain why.

9. Compare the work in this portfolio to the quizzes and tests you took on Greek mythology.

10. Which item in this portfolio was the most difficult for you to do? Why?

11. What are your goals for your next portfolio?

12. Which god or goddess from mythology would be considered the most "politically incorrect" if he/she lived in the 1990s in America? Why?

13

EXHIBITION IDEAS FOR PORTFOLIO

Location: _____*School Gym*_____ **Date:** *Oct. 20* **Time:** *10:00*

Who's Invited *Other classes, administration, parents, community members*

Description: Students and teachers dress up as their favorite character from Greek mythology. The students display their portfolios on tables as well as artifacts (posters, games, projects) they have done. Visitors are invited to talk with students and visit the four corners of the gym.

Corner #1—Refreshments – students serve ambrosia (mixed fruit), nectar (fruit juice), and grapes (food of the gods).

Corner #2—Video Corner – where copies of students' video skits and performances are shown.

Corner #3—Sports Corner – students demonstrate the athletic events that were included in the Olympic Games.

Corner #4—Music Corner – students present music of the Greeks using harps, lyres, and flutes. Groups perform Greek rap songs.

Culminating Event: Class presents original skit from mythology to group.

14

TABLE OF ACTIVITIES

Chapter 3: Select Key Artifacts

Chapter 4: Interject Personality

Chapter 5: Reflective Metacognitively

Chapter 6: Inspect to Self-Assess

How Does the Conference Happen?

Chapter 9: Inject/Eject to Update

Types

Chapter 10: Respect Accomplishments

Elements

BIBLIOGRAPHY

Archbald, D. A. & Newmann, F. M. (1988). *Beyond standardized testing: Assessing authentic achievement in secondary school.* Madison, WI: University of Wisconsin, National Association of Secondary School Principals.

Atwell, N. (1991). *Side by side: Essays on teaching to learn.* Portsmouth, NH: Heinemann, p. 3.

Bass, H. (1993, October 27). Let's measure what's worth measuring. *Education Week,* p.32.

Bellanca, J., Chapman, C., & Swartz, E. (1994). *Multiple assessments for multiple intelligences.* Palatine, IL: IRI/Skylight Publishing.

Belanoff, P., & Dickson, M. (1991). *Portfolios: Process and product.* Portsmouth, NH: Boyton & Cook Publishers.

Bower, B. E. (1994). *Assessment & evaluation: Mathematics in the transition years: A handbook for teachers of grade 9.* Durham, Ontario: Durham Board of Education.

Brooks, J., & Brooks, M. (1993). *In search of understanding: The case for constructivist classrooms.* Alexandria, VA: Association for Supervision and Curriculum Development.

Brown, R. (1989, April). Testing and thoughtfulness. *Educational Leadership,* pp. 31–33.

Burke, C. L. (1991, August). *Curriculum as inquiry.* Presentation at the Whole Language Umbrella Conference, Phoenix, AZ.

Burke, K. A. (1993). *The mindful school: How to assess authentic learning.* Palatine, IL: IRI/Skylight Publishing.

Burke, K.A. (Ed.). (1992). *Authentic assessment: A collection.* Palatine, IL: IRI/Skylight Publishing.

Campbell, J. (1992, May). Laser disk portfolios: Total child assessment. *Educational Leadership,* pp. 69–70.

Carnegie, D. (1981). *How to win friends and influence people.* New York: Simon and Schuster.

Chapman, C. (1993). *If the shoe fits . . . : How to develop multiple intelligences in the classroom.* Palatine, IL: IRI/Skylight Publishing.

Costa, A. L. (1993). Thinking: How do we know students are getting better at it? In K. A. Burke (Ed.), *Authentic assessment: A collection* (pp. 213–220). Palatine, IL: IRI/Skylight Publishing.

Costa, A. L. (1991). *The school as a home for the mind.* Palatine, IL: IRI/Skylight Publishing.

Costa, A. L., Bellanca, J., & Fogarty, R. (1992). *If minds matter: A foreword to the future,* Vol. I. Palatine, IL: IRI/Skylight Publishing.

Costa, A. L., Bellanca, J., & Fogarty, R. (1992). *If minds matter: A foreword to the future,* Vol. II. Palatine, IL: IRI/Skylight Publishing.

Crafton, L. (1994, April). Reflections. *Primary Voices*, pp. 39–42.

Crafton, L. (1991). *Whole language: Getting started . . . moving forward.* Katonah, NY: Richard C. Owen.

Crafton, L., & Burke, C. L. (1994, April). Inquiry-Based Evaluations: Teachers and Students Reflecting Together. *Primary Voices,* pp. 2–7.

Davies, A., Cameron, C., Politano, C., & Gregory, K. (1992). *Together is better: Collaborative assessment, evaluation & reporting.* Winnipeg, Canada: Pequis Publishers.

de Bono, E. (1992). *Serious creativity.* New York: HarperCollins.

Dietz, M. (1992). Professional development portfolio. In *Frameworks.* Shoreham, NY: California Professional Development Program.

Eisner, G. W. (1993, February). Why standards may not improve schools. *Educational Leadership,* pp. 22–23.

Ferrara, S., & McTighe, J. (1992). Assessment: A thoughtful process. In A. L. Costa, J. Bellanca, & R. Fogarty, (Eds.), *If minds matter: A foreword to the future,* Vol. II. (pp. 337–348). Palatine, IL: IRI/Skylight Publishing.

Flavell, J. H., Fredenchs, A. G., & Hoyt, J. D. (1970). Development changes in memorization processes. *Cognitive Psychology, 1*(4), pp. 324–340.

Fogarty, R. (1994). *The mindful school: How to teach for metacognitive reflection.* Palatine, IL: IRI/Skylight Publishing.

Fogarty, R. (1991). *The mindful school: How to integrate the curricula.* Palatine, IL: IRI/Skylight Publishing.

Fogarty, R., & Bellanca, J. (1989). *Patterns for thinking: Patterns for transfer.* Palatine, IL: IRI/Skylight Publishing.

Frazier, D. & Paulson, F. (1992, May). How portfolios motivate reluctant writers. *Educational Leadership,* pp. 62–65.

Fusco, E., & Fountain, A. (1992). Reflective teacher, reflective learner. In A. L. Costa, J. Bellanca, & R. Fogarty (Eds.), *If minds matter: A foreword to the future,* Vol. I. (pp. 239–255). Palatine, IL: IRI/Skylight Publishing.

Gardner, H. (1993). *Multiple intelligences: The theory in practice.* New York: HarperCollins.

Gardner, H. (1983). *Frames of mind: The theory of multiple intelligences.* New York: HarperCollins.

Glasser, W. (1986). *Control theory in the classroom.* New York: Harper and Row.

Glazer, S. M. (1993, December). How do I "grade" without grades? *Teaching K-8*, pp. 104–106.

Goodman, K., Bird, L. B., & Goodman, Y. M. (Eds.) (1992). *The whole language. Supplement on authentic assessment: Evaluating ourselves.* New York: SRA Macmillan/McGraw-Hill.

Hamm, M., & Adams, D. (1991, May). Portfolio: It's not just for artists anymore. *The Science Teacher*, pp. 18–21.

Hansen, J. (1992, May). Literacy portfolios: Helping students know themselves. *Educational Leadership*, pp. 66–68.

Harste, J. C., Woodward, V. A., & Burke, C. L. (1984). *Language stories and literacy lessons.* Portsmouth, NH: Heinemann.

Hebert, E. A. (1992, May). Portfolios invite reflection—from students *and* staff. *Educational Leadership*, pp. 61.

Herman, J. L., Aschbacher, P. R., & Winters, L. (1992). *A practical guide to alternative assessment.* Alexandria, VA: Association for Supervision and Curriculum Development.

Hill, B. C., & Ruptic, C. (1994). *Practical aspects of authentic assessment: Putting the pieces together.* Norwood, MA: Christopher-Gordon Publishers.

Hoff, R. (1992). *I can see you naked.* Kansas City, MO: Andrews and McMeel.

Howell, G. L., & Woodley, J. W. (1992). In K. S. Goodman, B. L. Bird, & Y. M. Goodman (Eds.), *The whole language supplement on authentic assessment: Evaluating ourselves* (p. 87). New York: SRA Macmillan/McGraw Hill.

Jalongo, M. R. (1992). Teachers' stories: Our ways of knowing. In K. A. Burke (Ed.), *Authentic assessment: A collection* (pp. 191–199). Palatine, IL: IRI/Skylight Publishing.

Jeroski, S. (1992). Finding out what we need to know. In A. L. Costa, J. Bellanca, & R. Fogarty (Eds.), *If minds matter: A foreword to the future,* Vol. II (pp. 281–295). Palatine, IL: IRI/Skylight Publishing.

Kallick, B. (1989). *Changing schools into communities for thinking.* Grandforks, ND: University of North Dakota Press.

Kamii, C., Clark, F. B., & Dominick, A. (1994, May). The six national goals: A road to disappointment. *Phi Delta Kappan*, pp. 672–677.

McDonald, J. P., Smith, S., Turner, D., Finney, M., & Barton, E. (1993). *Graduation by exhibition: Assessing genuine achievement.* Alexandria, VA: Association for Supervision and Curriculum Development.

Midwood, D., O'Connor, K., & Simpson, M. (1993). *Assess for success: Assessment, evaluation and reporting for successful learning.* Toronto, Ontario, Canada: Educational Services Committee, Ontario Secondary School Teachers' Federation.

Mills-Courts, K., & Amiran, M. R. (1991). Metacognition and the use of portfolios. In P. Belanoff, & M. Dickson (Eds.), *Portfolios: Process and product* (pp. 101–111). Portsmouth, NH: Baxton and Cook Publishers.

Paulson, F. L., Paulson, P. R., & Meyer, C. A. (1991, February). What makes a portfolio a portfolio? *Educational Leadership*, pp. 60–63.

Peter, L. J. (1977). *Peter's quotations: Ideas for our time.* New York: Bantam.

Silvers, P. (1994, April). Everyday signs of learning. *Primary Voices*, pp. 20–29.

Stefonek, T. (1991). *Alternative assessment: A national perspective.* Policy Briefs No. 15 & 16. Oak Brook, IL: North Central Regional Educational Laboratory.

Tchudi, S. (1991). *Planning and assessing the curriculum in English Language Arts.* Alexandria, VA: Association for Supervision and Curriculum Development.

Vavrus, L. (1990, August). Put portfolios to the test. *Instructor*, pp. 48–53.

Visovatti, K. (1994, April). Developing primary voices. *Primary Voices*, pp. 8–19.

Wiggins, G. (1994). *Standards, not standardization* [Videotape]. Distributed by Sunburst/Wings for Learning, 101 Castleton Street, P.O. Box 100, Pleasantville, NY 10570-0110.

Wolf, D. (1989, April). Portfolio assessment: Sampling student work. *Educational Leadership,* pp. 35–39.

Worthen, B. (1993, February). Critical issues that will determine the future of alternative assessment. *Phi Delta Kappan*, pp. 444–456.

Zimmerman, J., (Ed.). (1993, November). Student portfolios: Classroom uses. *Research Education Consumer Guide*, Number 8, p.1.

INDEX

NOTES

NOTES

NOTES

NOTES

NOTES

LEARN FROM OUR BOOKS
AND FROM OUR AUTHORS!
Bring Our Author-Trainers to Your District

Now that you have benefited from IRI/Skylight's high-quality publications, extend your learning by meeting the actual authors. IRI/Skylight authors are seasoned professionals with a wealth of knowledge and experience. They offer dynamic, exciting presentations. Many authors are available to visit your site and discuss their particular areas of expertise!

Training of Trainers

IRI provides comprehensive inservice training for experienced educators who are qualified to train other staff members. IRI presenters possess years of experience at all levels of education and include authors, field experts, and administrators. IRI/Skylight's training of trainers program is the most powerful and cost-effective way to build the skills of your entire staff.

Training Programs

IRI/Skylight training is available in your district or intermediate agency. Gain practical techniques and strategies for implementing the latest findings from educational research. No matter the topic, IRI/Skylight has an experienced consultant who can design and specially tailor an inservice to meet the needs of your school or organization.

Network

An IRI/Phi Delta Kappa partnership, _The Network of Mindful Schools_ is a program of site-based systemic change, built on the core values advocated by Arthur Costa. Each member school is committed to restructuring itself to become a "home for the mind." The network is built on three elements: a site leader, a faculty that functions as a team, and an external support system to aid in school transformation.

To receive a free copy of the IRI/Skylight Catalog, find out more about The Network of Mindful Schools, or for more information about trainings offered by IRI/Skylight, contact:

IRI/Skylight Publishing, Inc.
200 E. Wood Street, Suite 274, Palatine, Illinois 60067
800-348-4474
FAX 708-991-6420

There are

one-story intellects,

two-story intellects, and three-story

intellects with skylights. All fact collectors, who have

no aim beyond their facts, are one-story men. Two-story men

compare, reason, generalize, using the labors of the fact collectors as

well as their own. Three-story men idealize, imagine,

predict—their best illumination comes from

above, through the skylight.

—*Oliver Wendell*

Holmes